Armando P. Ribas

Rule of Law: the Path to Freedom

༜ - STOCKCERO - ༜

Copyright © Armando P. Ribas
of this edition © Stockcero 2012
1st. Stockcero edition: 2012

ISBN: 978-1-934768-51-8

Library of Congress Control Number: 2012933039

All rights reserved.
This book may not be reproduced, stored in a retrieval system, or transmitted, in whole or in part, in any form or by any means, electronic, mechanical, photocopying, recording, or otherwise, without written permission of Stockcero, Inc.

Set in Linotype Granjon font family typeface
Printed in the United States of America on acid-free paper.

Published by Stockcero, Inc.
3785 N.W. 82nd Avenue
Doral, FL 33166
USA
stockcero@stockcero.com

www.stockcero.com

Armando P. Ribas

Rule of Law: the Path to Freedom

Contents

Foreword 7
I. Political Philosophy
1. The Ethical Conditions of Freedom...15
2. Civilization and Rational Barbarism 17
3. Some Reflections to Find the Path to Freedom 24
4. Ethics and Liberty 36
5. The Rule of Law and True Democracy in the World 47
6. Liberalism and the Nation 49
7. The Exceptionalism of the United States.................................55

II. Roman Law and the Rule of Law
1. Natural Law and Positive Law..61
2. The Judiciary Power 66
3. Ius Gentium and Codification 68
4. The American Legal System 71

III. Syndicalism and Individual Rights
1. Types of Syndicalism..75
2. The Rights of Association in Argentina 76
3. Syndicalism in the United States of America 80
4. Socialism, Communism and Syndicates...................................82
5. Syndicalism and «Justicialismo» 84
6. The Legislation in Force and its Antecedents in the Light of the Constitutional Principles 88

IV. Foreign Policy
1. Western Ethics and the Environment......................................93
2. Intellectuals and Globalization..97
3. Marx and Human Rights...101
4. Obama, the Founding Fathers and the New Man 105
5. From the Cold War to the Hot Peace 110

6. Latin American Democracies at Bay 116
7. The Road to Liberate Latin America from Its Liberators 120
8. The Business of Benevolence and Latin American Fantasies 131
9. Drugs, Revolution and the Colombian Plan 135
10. Theocracy and Ratiocracy...138
11. Between Cowboys and Jacobins..143
12. The Huntington's Challenge to Civilization 149
13. Bonjour Tristese 155

V. Economics
1. Liberalism and Financial Crisis..159
2. Conference at the Council of the Americas 164
3. Moral Hazard or Political Hazard 170
4. The Dynamics of the Disequilibrium..173
5. The Nordic Countries 176
6. The Mexican Case 178
7. The Argentine Dilemma 180
8. Argentina on the Threshold 185
9. Banking Crisis and the Argentine Experience 189
10. The Washington Consensus vs. the Philadelphia Consensus 206
11. Public Debt and IMF 210
12. Sustainable Development and the Precautionary Principle 221

Foreword

There is a great confusion in the world and even more in that part of the world that considers itself as representing the Western civilization. This confusion arises in two realms: the semantic one and the conceptual one. The first of these confusions is the result of ignoring the ethical and the political philosophy antithesis between the Anglo-American philosophy and the Franco-German one. As Balint Vazsonyi once wrote, they are as different as day and night.

At the same time, that philosophical confusion to which I refer as the syncretism of Western philosophy is the pretentious nirvana of democracy in the West. Conceptually, democracy may be divided in two antithetical systems: the rule of law and the majority rule. Majority rule is the opposite of the protection of individual rights: to life, liberty, property and the pursuance of happiness.

The apparent right of the majorities is no more than the absolute power of governments in the name of the people, that is, the new deity. In Aristotelian terms, that is demagoguery and that is why democracy fails in Latin America, and so it was in Europe, where Hitler and Mussolini represented majority rule as the most common name: reason of the state.

In Europe, since the times of Montesquieu and with the decided influence of Rousseau, democracy has been confused with socialism under the aegis of equality. Equality under the law is the opposite of that sort of equality which in socialism leads to the arbitrariness of government, which appears to be representing the ethics of the society against private interests. The left has taken advantage of monopolizing the ethics of the society against the materialism of private interest. That is, the assumption that private interests are against general interests becomes the excuse for socialism and the violation of the rule of law, that is, the limit of political power.

Unfortunately, the acceptance that democracy is the result of universal suffrage and capitalism is the materialism of the private interest is the cause that the left has done what Rush Limbaugh have called «political cleansing» and monopolize the ethics of society in the name of equality. The United States has helped to this misunderstanding. In the first place, because instead of recognizing its own system as the rule of law it has accepted the legitimacy of democracy as universal suffrage. At the same time, it has devalued the implicit liberalism of *The Federalist Papers* by calling liberals to the socialists. On the other hand, the system of the rule of law had been called «capitalism» by Marx. In that sense, the systems become the realm of materialism through the two Marxist approaches: the alienation and the theory of exploitation. Hence the left appears to be the moral defense of the people violating individual rights.

The history of mankind has been dramatic or even tragic. War was always the reason of states. In such a world ignorance and lack of information was the natural character of societies. So poverty, sloth and barbarism prevailed for more than five thousand years. The very idea of freedom was alien to humanity where work was slavery and trade was despicable until very recently. Our own world as perceived from the past could not be more than a utopia; however, we seem to have a romantic perception of that past at the time that we disqualify the present in ethical terms.

This ethical approach to the past while pretending in a rousseaunian way that «our souls have been corrupted in proportion as our sciences and arts have advanced toward perfection» hinders any possibility to understand the world we live in. Notwithstanding that romantic view of the past, we are accepting an image of the so-called Western civilization as a coalition of Christian virtue and the reason of the Enlightenment. Consequently, we are ignoring the deep ethical antagonism prevailing within our own Western society, regardless the antagonism with the Moslem world.

It was Karl Popper who in his essay «The History of Our Time: An Optimist's View» wrote, «I assert that our own free world is by far the best society which has come into existence during the course of human history». There is no doubt that in spite of the present difficulties, the world has improved since that relatively recent time. It is not only important to recognize the wonders of the present world, but it is even more important to understand the actual causes of this historical achievement.

The first thing that we have to admit is that there was not a secular historical advance of the world. The history of mankind shows fairly clear that there was a turning point in time, and from then on the economy and the population started to grow. Let me remind the simple analysis of Simon Kuznets on this subject. In his *Modern Economic Growth*, he wrote, «If per capita product had grown 15 percent per decade for three centuries before the 1960s, per capita product in the 1660s would have been $1/66^{th}$ of the present level. But a per capita income at even a twentieth of the present levels could not have sustained the population of even the most developed countries; and the assumed rates of growth in per capita product could not have been maintained in most countries for more than two centuries».

It might seem surprising that even Karl Marx agrees with the above conclusion, and so he said in *The Communist Manifesto*, published in 1848, «The bourgeoisie, during its rule of scarcely one hundred years, has created more massive and more colossal productive forces than have all preceding generations together». Hence we may conclude that the economic growth or the perfection of arts and sciences did not start before 1750.

Evidently the causes which determined this advance were not economic as such, but economic growth was the consequence of deep changes in ethical and political ideas. We may say then that the so-called Industrial Revolution actually was a philosophical and ethical revolution, which took into account man frailty as the starting point to organize political society. So David Hume said that given the fact that human nature was unchangeable, in order to change behavior it was necessary to change circumstances. That was what took place in England after the Glorious Revolution of 1688, under the aegis of Locke's thinking, who discovered that monarchs were also men.

Those principles were carried out even further by the Americans somewhat later, and in that respect allow me to quote Ira Glasser, who wrote, «The early Americans did indeed invent a new form of government. But they did more than that: they declared a new purpose for government. That new purpose was the protection of individual rights. No government had ever before been created primarily for that purpose. Before 1787, the role of government was assumed to be the enforcement of community consensus aimed at making citizen virtuous and moral». In other words, Americans learnt Locke and Hume's approach to human nature in order to organize government accordingly under the Rule of Law. Nothing of that sort ever happened in continental Europe, where the French Revolution and the Enlightenment were the intellectual sources of the totalitarian systems that developed during the twentieth century.

My contention then is that the Anglo-American political philosophy is not the product of any particular religious belief or any race. If Weber's theories respecting the protestant capitalist ethics were right, then the Industrial Revolution should have taken place originally in Germany, which was the cradle of Protestantism, and not England, where the break up with the Pope had sexual and economic connotation rather than theological. It was not either the result of a racial component, because even after Anglicanism prevailed during the Tudors, Great Britain continued being a poor country, where there was no freedom. David Hume, in his *History of England*, describes the situation in the following way, «The English in that age were so thoroughly subdued that like the Eastern slaves, they were inclined to admire those acts of violence and tyranny, which were exercised over themselves and at their own expense». And with respect to the Cromwell's revolution, he said, «England had never known a more severe and arbitrary government than was generally exercised by the patrons of liberty».

By the same token, Germany continued being one of the most backward countries of Europe until the second half of the nineteenth century, where there was not freedom either. In spite of this fact, the world has had to suffer the philosophical influence of the Germans, from Kant, Hegel, Fichte, Herder and Nietzsche to finally Marx and Engels. Hence freedom has been the consequence of ethical and philosophical principles, which are the antithesis of the rationalist and romantic approach which ended up in nationalism and socialism, where the realism of the universals determines the actual violation of individual rights in the name of the common good. The best example of this conclusion is the development of Argentina during the second half of the nineteenth century, when she accepted the validity of those principles.

Then it is obvious that besides the Islamic terrorism, there is a deep ethical antagonism within the West. As Von Mises said in 1952, the problem with socialism is that even those who oppose it are willing to accept its essential ethical premises. At the same time that the people seem to decry the values which determined the improvement of the word as selfish and materialistic, they pretend to convert the good and the services so created in universal human rights.

Most unfortunately, I can say that the true antagonism in the world is not cultural or religious, but ideological. Socialist values are accepted as such, both by religious beliefs as well as by the romantic rationalism. In order to understand the reality that we are facing in the world today, it is necessary to understand this historical ethical and philosophical antagonism, and to achieve that understanding has been and still is my quest.

I. Political Philosophy

1. The Ethical Conditions of Freedom

Since I was forced to leave Cuba, I have considered that my main mission in this world is the fight for freedom. Since 1960 I have written thousands of articles on the subject which have been published in different important newspapers including *The Wall Street Journal*, *La Nación*, *La Prensa*, *El Cronista Comercial*, *El País* (Uruguay), *The Miami Herald* and more lately el *Diario Las Américas*. At the same time, I have published 15 books, among them: *Entre la Libertad y la Servidumbre*, *¿Quién es Occidente?*, *Argentina, un Milagro de la Historia*, *Cuba Entre la Independencia y la Libertad*, and others. In the last fifteen years, I have directed a TV program (*Sin Fronteras*) devoted to defend the main principles of freedom.

It is my understanding that in the world exists an increasing confusion concerning the values that changed the history of mankind. Freedom as it is now known was completely ignored throughout history, while war and oppression were the actual name of the game. It was only in the last 250 years that a change in ethical values produced a turning point in history. However, the benefits arising from that change in values are more and more being taken for granted, while the principles that changed the world are not only ignored but, worse than that, disqualified as the product of man selfishness, as against generosity and solidarity.

Even Karl Marx recognized that wealth in the world had not started before the eighteenth century. However, it was he who more profoundly disqualified the system that produced it, as the result of the exploitation of the workers by the capitalists. Unfortunately, even after the crumbling of the Berlin Wall, the socialist approach prevails in the majority of the countries on the assumption of the struggle for equality.

The purpose of the work that I am presenting to you is to help to understand the change in values that determined a turning point in the history of mankind. One of the main confusions still prevailing is the ethical assumption of the Western Civilization as the result of the confluence of Greek philosophy and Christian ethics. My main contention is that there is not such a thing as a univocal ethics as the Western Civilization, but, on the contrary, it has been within the West where the two antithetical political philosophies arose, The Anglo-American and the Franco- German. The first produced the reign of freedom while the second produced the totalitarian systems as the rationalization of despotism.

It is my purpose then to try to clarify this confusion in order to save the world for freedom. As Thomas Sowell said, «Dangers to a society may be mortal without being immediate». And one of the main dangers that is threatening our continent is the belief that majority rule should prevail over individual and minority rights. It is my hope that with this essay I may be able to help to better understand the world we live in in order to save mankind for freedom, which is more and more threatening by the striving for equality. The present antagonism in the world is not racial, cultural or religious but conceptually ethical.

2. Civilization and Rational Barbarism

Those who still believe that the rift between France and Germany on one side and the United States on the other is due to the different approaches of how to deal with Saddam Hussein do not know the history of Europe or the United States. It would be worthwhile to ask ourselves why a country which was born at the end of the eighteenth century could surpass a continent which, according to Hegel, monopolized universal history.

It is understandable, on the other hand, that a continent where war has been the name of the game for centuries and so it has suffered its horrors could be reluctant to face another one. From that point of view, pacifism is not only understandable but also valuable. However, we should remember Clausewitz dictum, «If you wish peace be prepared for war». It is apparent though that the major discrepancy between the two contenders with respect to Iraq is not the objective of disarming Saddam but the «timing».

Why then is it that if timing is the potential reason for discord there is such a deep confrontation between the parties involved? Even more we may see that Saddam has achieved the division of the West, as much as a breakdown of NATO. The truth of the matter is that the European Union was the outcome of the threat of the Evil Empire and NATO. We should remember that Napoleon had said that the unification of Europe would come as soon as a Mongol's hair tail could show behind the Urals. Actually, it was not the hair tail of a Mongol but the excrescence of the Marxist dialectical rationalism, what caused about the same result. That «hair tail» sealed the Atlantic Alliance, and the world was confused by the wrong notion of the so-called Western Civilization.

But what is Europe? According to G. R. Elton, up to the fifteenth century, Europe was recalled as Zeus' lover, who faking as a bull flew her hiding from Athena. The Asian Western peninsula called itself as the Christendom, as I wrote some time ago, Christians killed among themselves, but loving each other. In the ninth century, it was the final break-up between Rome and Bizancio with the help of Charles the Great. At the time, Bizancio was the most civilized remnant of the Roman Empire after its fall due to the collusion between the Huns and the Christians. The Crusades organized with the apparent purpose of rescuing the Holly took the time to destroy Bizancio on the way and it finally disappeared when Christ was replaced by Allah and his prophet Mohammed under the Ottoman's aegis.

In 1517, the profitable stock operation «in plenary indulgences» provoked the ire of an Augustinian monk, Martin Luther, against real estate operation in heaven. This process allowed the German prince to appropriate Rome's real property on earth. A little later, Calvin gave God what is due to God and the traders what belong to the traders and so watches and clocks appeared. On the other side of the British Channel, a Blue Beard predecessor, at the time nominated «defender of the faith», Henry VIII, decided not to pay the dues to Rome. In the meantime, he took advantage of the occasion to initiate the *vincular* divorce by *desvinculating* the head from the body of his wives. Then Anne Boleyn came, and she gave life to the virgin queen who, with the help of the elements, defeated the undefeatable armada which had not been sent to fight against the elements.

In 1618, the love among the Christians was proven in the Thirty Year War, which with religious seal eliminated half of the population of Europe without nuclear weapons. In 1648, those Lord lovers decided to end this holocaust and signed the Peace of Westphalia, according to which each prince was allowed to impose its particular communication with God to his subjects. Christian brotherhood was recognized then.

On the other side of the British Channel, the sea had saved the British from the continental holocaust and, in the meantime, the Scottish, the Stuarts, rose to the British crown and apparently they tried again to pay its due to the Church of Rome. As charity started at home, it claimed the presence of the Lord Protector, Mr Oliver Cromwell, to resist that ecclesiastic return. So in proper defense of the

Parliament and the religion of the British subjects, as it had been organized by the virgin queen through the Court of High Commission, it was decided the decapitation of Charles I for such a heresy. Afterwards, he took care of the Parliament and in its building he placed an advertisement saying «For Rent without Furniture» following the steps of the Tudors, who had ignored Magna Carta for more than 100 years.

It was taking advantage of that European situation of loving your neighbor in order to send them to the side of the Lord that some prudent materialists influenced by their desire to remain longer in this valley of tears crossed the Atlantic in the Mayflower. Fortunately for the British, John Locke was born in 1632 and his *Letter of Tolerance (A Letter Concerning Toleration)* and the *First and Second Treatises of Civil Government* established for the first time the fundamental principles of free government. These principles were institutionalized during the Glorious Revolution, in 1688, and in this way the concept of freedom was born in the world as reckoned by the limitation to political power, the separation of Church from State and the individual rights to life, liberty, property and the pursuance of men to their own happiness. It was established then a new relation between the citizens and the government, whose function is the defense of such individual rights.

On the continent, it was the «moral» figure of Jean Jacques Rousseau who after abandoning his wife and five children, established the moral principles in order to save men from slavery and return them to the state of nature. I do not know if it was on account of Voltaire's criticism or Rousseau's despise for arts and science that he changed his original romanticism for a rational approach contained in his *Social Contract* to force men to be free through the sovereignty of the general will. This is the beginning of the Enlightenment and the rational morality to create the new man; the guillotine on behalf of liberty, equality and fraternity by the hand of the incorruptible Maximiliem Robespierre decapitated from right to right and blame the bakers for the raising of the bread's price.

Reason replaced faith, and the committees for public health took the place of the Inquisition in its moral endeavor on earth. Then the French Revolution appears in the eyes of humanity as the continuation of the other one which had taken place on the other side of the Atlantic based on complete different principles and the aegis of «no taxation without representation». That revolution, which was the final outcome of that stormy trip of the Mayflower, was expressed in the Constitution of 1787 and the Bill of Rights in 1791. In *The Federalist Papers*, Madison and Hamilton recognized the philosophical principles of freedom as expressed by Locke, Hume, Adam Smith, Burke, etcetera, and the individual rights took juridical character through John Marshal in the case Marbury vs. Madison.

The system of controlling the government established through the fundamental role of the Supreme Court in order to guarantee individual rights constitutes the major reason for the superiority of the United States over Europe. Meanwhile, in the continent, the Enlightenment defined by Kant as man's emergence of his self-incurred immaturity taught *sapere aude* and so reason took the place of God. What I have denominated «reason obscurantism», that is, rationalism coupled to romanticism as the universalization of individual feelings, constituted the base of the totalitarianism system of fascism, nazism and communism, which set asunder the world during the twentieth century. So nationalism is coupled to socialism in the rational morality of the universals to ignore the individual rights under the reason of state. As it was stated by Ayn Rand, individual rights had been ignored in Europe up to our times.

Based on reason from the Enlightenment came Rousseau, Babeuf, Comte, Kant, Fichte, Nietzsche, Herder, Hegel, Marx, etcetera. In that way, Europe went from the Holly Inquisition to the committees of public health in the hand of the Jacobins to the holocaust Nazi and the Bolsheviks gulags. Notwithstanding these horrors, the intellectual arrogance developed a value category, the Western civilization as the way of reason in history towards the kingdom of freedom. In this way, the deep ethical philosophical division between the Anglo-American political philosophy and the Franco-Germanic one was ignored, as it was clearly expressed by Balint Vazsonyi in his *Americas' 30 Years War*.

From this historical confusion after the crumbling of the Berlin wall came out the Fukuyama theory of the definitive triumph of liberal democracy and the end of history as had been forecasted by a «republican» Hegel who I do not know. From this erroneous thesis came through the communications the so-called globalization, which is the assumed establishment of liberal democracies in the world. It was ignored then that we had globalized information whereas the formation which had produced the modern world was ignored and despised not only in the countries of the third world but precisely in the European Union, where still prevails the reason of state in the hands of social democracy. Another fallacious theory was presented by Mr Huntington, according to which a new antagonism was to develop among civilizations. Mr Huntington did not know that as Václav Havel said, there is only one civilization even when there could be multiple cultures. Civilization is the kingdom of individual freedom and where there is no such freedom there is no civilization.

Today the European unification as pretended by France and Germany, which apparently responds to the difference in timing with respect to Iraq, does not come out as Napoleon had foreseen it. It will not be the product of the hair tail of a Mongol behind the Urals but of the cowboy hat floating in the Atlantic. The European unification comes then not from the convenience of a common market to improve the lives of the Europeans so much historically hurt by their own government but as a project to antagonize politically with their savers. In other words, in order to face the civilization not from the religious fundamentalism but from the rationalist romantic fundamentalism, which is the base of social democracy.

When the unification of Europe is assertively present in order to balance the power of the civilizing super power, Europe again finds its make historical course. I should say, however, that we have to a fundamental distinction. There were France and Germany from the time of Richelieu, Louis XIV, the Convention, Napoleon, Bismarck, the Kaiser and Hitler, the greatest oppressors and predators of Europe. Eastern Europe, with Poland and the Czech Republic at the helm, was never considered as part of the Western civilization as much as Spain, Portugal and Italy, the European countries which have shown a better understanding of the nature of the antagonism. Terror today is fed by Franco-Germanic, the inconsistency with respect to the peril posed by the medieval availability of the world technology of the third millennium. Then, I believe that we can perceive the wisdom of Adam Smith when he said, «It was not the wisdom and policy, but the disorder and injustice of the European governments which peopled and cultivated America». Hence, allow me to suggest creating an Atlantic Alliance between America and the European countries which built it, that is, England, Spain and Portugal. A world in which civilization reigns without reason of the state and founded injustice as the final expression of the limits of political power. The universal project should be individual freedom.

3. Some Reflections to Find the Path to Freedom

In 1910 Luis Alberto de Herrera wrote a book, *La Revolución Francesa y Sudamérica* (*The French Revolution and South America*), and there he said, «The inflexible dogmas of the French Revolution commanded to collide against reality. On its behalf and in order every South American society has fallen and continues falling in the abyss of institutional fraud, which leads to the civil war». *Mutatis mutandis* this observation more than explains the continuing failures of democratic processes in Latin America during the twentieth century which appear to continue in the third millennium.

Evidently, as Herrera had discovered, our historical failures result from the original error of confusing the American Revolution with the French Revolution, which were actually antithetical. What is more, we also ignored the so-called Glorious Revolution of 1688 in Great Britain led by the sounds principles of John Locke as expressed in his *Second Treatise of Civil Government* as well as the *Letter Concerning Tolerance*. Hence, democracy in Latin America under the aegis of the *Social Contract* was the realm of majority rule ignoring the major achievement of civilization, which was the recognition of individual rights: «life, liberty, property and the pursuance of happiness».

The alternative to the *Social Contract* which through the *Communist Manifest* led to communism was the *Leviathan* that was represented as expressed by Thomas Hobbes by the state which was the «mortal god as inspired by the immortal God». Latin America then changed through its independence from the divine rights of monarchs to the divine rights of people. No one realized the important finding of Locke respecting the apparently historically ignored fact that monarchs were also men. So he wrote, «But I shall desire those who make this objection to remember that absolute monarchs are but men». But even more transcendental to understand the Latin American political experience is his wise observation respecting political power as such. And so he said, «Hence it is a mistake to think that the supreme or legislative power of any common wealth can do what it will and dispose of the estates of the subjects arbitrarily or take any part of them at pleasure».

That was the confusion which Juan Bautista Alberdi explained so wisely in his *Conferencia de Luz del Día (Conference of Luz del Día)* between external freedom (independence) and domestic freedom as individual freedom. So he said, «What is the condition of the Latin liberty? It is the liberty of all refunded and consolidated in one single collective and solidary liberty, which is exclusively exorcised by an emperor or a liberator czar. It is the liberty of the country personalized in the government and the entire government personalized in one man». That is why Alberdi suggested, «South America will be free when it becomes free from its liberators».

Evidently the father of the Argentine Constitution of 1853 had realized the difference between the Franco-German political philosophy and the Anglo-American one, which, as Balint Vazsonyi sustained, are as different as day and night. Unfortunately, not even at this stage of history we have realized this obvious opposition and we insist on the fallacy of shared values in the history of Western Civilization. Argentina in 1853 chose the Anglo-American political philosophy and in only fifty years developed as the eighth richest country in the world at the beginning of the twentieth century. That was not the case of the rest of the Latin American countries, which continued torn between the *Leviathan* and the *Social Contract*.

My major concern is that not only Latin America ignores the opposition between these philosophies but that the whole world appears to have this philosophical confusion as the so-called globalization becomes the new philosophy of history, which in terms of Fukuyama has led to the end of history. But we should remember that it was Emmanuel Kant, who in his essay «What is Enlightenment?» said, «Enlightenment is man emergence from his self-incurred immaturity. Immaturity is the inability to use one's own understanding without the guidance of another. The motto of Enlightenment is therefore *Sapere Aude*. Have courage to use your own understanding». Unfortunately, from that very motto surged what I have called the «obscurantism of reason». That is, Cartesian rationalism which postulated that at the end reason was the unfailing way to truth. From then on came the Kantian reason in history aside from reason in men's minds and ended up with the Hegelian dialectical process in which reason *per se* closed the gap between reality and rationality.

On the other side of the British Channel, a different approach to the validity of reason gave rise to a completely different and opposing view over human nature. Reason was another imperfect instrument to the difficult road to knowledge, which is always contingent. As Hume had said, «It is from the non-rational elements of our minds that men are saved from total skepticism». Then, we can see that from the very source of superseding immaturity surged a different approach which motto could be *non sapere aude*. That is, to acknowledge that we live in a world of uncertainty and that men's frailty is a fact of nature and not the lack of courage to know.

Recent history as developed throughout the twentieth century showed how these two opposing views of the world developed in the final antagonism between freedom and servitude. The Franco-German political philosophy arising from *sapere aude* or what I have called the «obscurantism of reason» gave rise to the oppressive ideologies of Nazism, Fascism and Marxism (Communism). On the other hand, liberal democracy prevailed through the Anglo-American political philosophy under the consciousness of men fallibility.

Unfortunately, the demise of Communism in the Soviet Empire in no way determined the disappearance of Marxism. Social democracy is Marxism through Bernstein rather than Lenin. Hence we can see that in Europe now including Great Britain through the Labor Party, social democracy and not liberal democracy is the new name of the game. Eduard Bernstein, who should be included as a «master thinker» as the *nouvelle droite* called the German philosophers, wrote the main tenets of social democracy. In *The Preconditions of Socialism*, Bernstein wrote, «Socialism was the legitimate heir of liberalism... There is no really liberal thought which does not also belong to the elements of the ideas of socialism». This is the greatest mistake of social democracy, because socialism is not the heir of liberalism but its antithesis, as Marx very well explained.

Liberalism in the Anglo-American philosophy is an ethical approach to society based on the awareness of the fallibility of human nature. It is for that very reason that liberalism proposes the limits to political power as a safeguard of individual rights. In that sense, civilization is a learning process of controlling the base passions of humanity through justice and property. It is not the reason in history as a fateful process of liberty based on the improvement of human nature. Socialism, on the other hand, is conceived as the historical process of liberation in order to overcome scarcity. This is the Marxian approach and it was later admitted by Bernstein himself.

That is what I have called «the syncretism of Western philosophy» and which has politically developed in the so-called human rights. This divinization of humanity as such ignores man's fallibility as recognized by the gospel. In this process, private interests are anathematized, and the state, as the representative of general interest, becomes in Hegelian terms the «Divine idea as it exists on earth...». This concept, according to which the state monopolized morality, means that all idea of limited political power is actually precluded. By the same token, this monopolization of social morality by the state means the actual power of bureaucracy to violate individual rights in order to achieve equality through social rights. Hence the philosophical syncretism was politically transformed into the intermingling of individual rights and their opposite, the social rights, or social privileges granted by political power.

The striving for equality through the manipulation of social rights has produced the worst political mistake, which in the end means the legitimation of violence in the name of income equalization. As Karl Popper had said, «Utopianism is self-defeating and it leads to violence». In my view, this political utopianism comes out of three different sources. The first one is religious fanaticism; the second one is rationalism, which is what I have called the «obscurantism of reason». That is the pretension that reason *per se* equals truth. And the third one is political romanticism, which ignores Hume's dictum respecting the fact that there is not such a thing as the love to human kind. Love is a particular feeling, and political romanticism is the universalization of such feeling, as a categorical imperative. I may add a fourth source, which is the ignorance of the people and the natural tendency of envy. That is why I have sustained that the so-called globalization can hardly tend to unified system of common interest, because what people learn through communications is precisely the huge differences in wealth and not its determinant. Little by little, the original European confusion between democracy and socialism as developed since Montesquieu degenerated into the political mess which has affected democracy in Latin America.

As had been brilliantly perceived by Herrera, that French philosophical and political muddle as rationalized by the «Master Thinkers» has produced the going on civil war, which worst result was the Cuban Revolution. Another illuminating book by the Venezuelan Carlos Rangel, *From the Good Savage to the Good Revolutionary* (*Del buen salvaje al buen revolucionario*), describes the political mythology which García Márquez defines as magic realism. But Rangel knows better that we did not invent the myths but inherited them from Europe and so he says, «The fundamental myths of America are not absolutely Americans. They are myths created by the European imagination or they even came from afar from the Judeo-Greek antiquity...».

Cuba, in my opinion, was not an exception in Latin America, but the final outcome of this political mythology confronted with reality, which ended in civil war. The difference is that in Cuba the guerrillas defeated the army, that was the exception. But actually it was not. In my view, there are two main reasons that explain why Cuba fell under communism. Cuba had enjoyed a very special economic relationship with the United States, which saved her from the poverty that other Latin American countries were and continue experiencing on account of their own ignorance with respect to the main tenets of a Republic, which are individual rights. The stupidity was the same but, thanks to the Americans, we did not pay for it. So the main reason of our support of Castro's anti-Americanism was the gap between our relative wealth and the lack of knowledge respecting the reasons that provided it. We believed to be above the other Latin Americans and of course we assumed that we could challenge the greatest civilization ever achieved in the history of mankind with no cost. The second determinant of this fatal destiny was the fact that Sergeant Fulgencio Batista y Zaldívar had decapitated the Cuban army in 1933. The sergeants became generals and got power with the support of the revolutionaries. In 1959, the sergeants turned the power back to the revolutionaries thinking that they were going to share it, but actually they lost their heads. The United States had two opportunities to revert this setback to Western civilization, but the New Frontier with Mr John Fitzgerald Kennedy at the helm decided to exchange crocodiles for missiles in what Paul Johnson defined as the «America's suicide attempt».

The lesson was learned in the rest of the continent, where the army notwithstanding their political weaknesses had been the one and only safeguard against the communist assault. At the same time, once and again the guerrillas lost the war against the Army in Latin America, the left under the umbrella of the European social democracy is winning the peace and the so-called populism appears to be the alternative to the economic failure of the pejorative misnomer of neoliberalism. That is the democratic attempt to liberalize and stabilize the economy and privatize the state enterprises.

Apparently nobody tries even to recognize that the only Latin American exception to this democratic failure has been the Chilean case. While Castro remains the very symbol of anti-imperialism, General Pinochet has hardly overcome the Europeans attempts to imprison him while forgetting their own historical sins. His main fault was that he succeeded while all the other military governments failed. The left once again has succeeded in confusing the minds of the people, associating the militaries with the right and the right with capitalism and the collusion with imperialism. In Europe they had succeeded in confusing aristocracy with capitalism when actually it was through capitalism that aristocracy lost power. Trade and labor, which are the determinants of wealth, replaced war as the main object of the state.

We insist, however, on ignoring that the aristocratic character rests on the assumption that distribution and not wealth creation is the foundation of ethics. So we come back to square one, and private interest is *a priori* considered to be contrary to the so-called common good, and that efficient production is pure materialism while distribution through political power is somehow spiritualism. So Hegel is back, and the increase in government expenditures is the economic outcome of that ethical approach.

The irruption of the militaries in the political arena of Latin America and in particular the inflation were considered the political and economic maladies which destroyed the natural well-being which the Latin American deserved. The recovery of democracy and the stabilization process that followed during the nineties, while Latin America collapsed under political upheavals and deep recession, showed the fallacy of such assumption.

The political problem was not the militaries as such in the same way that inflation was not the economic problem. The militaries as well as the inflation were the consequence of a deeper political and ethical problem which is the lack of juridical security. That is the ignorance of the rule of law which is the respect of individual rights. Unfortunately, the European example is more and more the main problem faced by the world and in particular the Latin American countries which tend to be a farce of the European tragedy. While the European economies, including France, Italy and Germany, collapse under the burden of an overwhelming welfare state, protectionism is again the main threat to the world economy. Socialism is a very expensive way of producing, and protectionism appears to be the only wise and ethical political solution. If the developed economies are under social democracy it is not difficult to imagine that such a recipe is the main stumbling block to development.

The failure of the so-called neoliberalism was not the opening of the economy, or the privatization process as the left pretends to be, but the impossibility to control government expenditures on the one hand, and the inflexibility of the labor system. As long as we continue believing that distribution is ethical whereas the creation of wealth and profits is materialism, the producers of poverty will always get the votes to be in power. It is the very appeal to the distribution of wealth the main cause of the unequal distribution of wealth as well as the pauperization which comes about as a consequence not of capitalism but of the corruption implied in socialism. As Marx had brilliantly explained in his criticism to Hegel's *Theory of the State*, the bureaucrats convert their own private interest into general interests. Unfortunately, the so-called globalization is a fallacy and the communications have globalized information but not formation. That is the very system that produces the wealth which is known through the communication system that is not only ignored but resented by the majority of the countries in the world and not least by the European Union, where social democracy prevails.

Then, it is very important to understand the real nature of the failure of the so-called neoliberalism, because otherwise the left will succeed in reverting to populism and violence. This lesson has to be learnt more than anyone else by the IMF, which dogmatic approach to adjustment and monetary and fiscal equilibrium has been unable to solve the recent financial crisis in the world. I may say then that, as George Gilder explained in his *Wealth and Poverty*, government expenditures are not part of the product, but a factor of production, that is, part of the cost of producing. Coming back to basics, macroeconomic theory has forgotten the fundamental source of wealth, which is microeconomic and so Gilder says, «Sooner or later, the American liberals like the British Laborites are going to discover that monetary restriction is a wonderful way to destroy the private sector while leaving government intact and offering pretexts for nationalizing industry. Since government has become a factor of production, the only way to diminish its impact on prices is to economize on it just as one would economize on the use of land, labor or capital by reducing its size or increasing its productivity». And then, he continued saying, «It is not principally the federal deficit that causes inflation. If the deficit were closed by higher tax rates and the money supply were held constant the price level would likely rise in the orthodox way of the law of cost». I would add that interest rates will also rise, and a fundamental disequilibrium would be created as market interest rates are above the profitability of the business sector or what Keynes called «the marginal efficiency of capital».

In Argentina, we have experienced once and again the

deleterious results of the attempts to compensate the increase in government expenditures by higher taxes, monetary control and a fixed nominal exchange rate. The last experience of the so-called convertibility has been worse because it lasted longer, and while inflation is an equilibrating process of disequilibrium, the real interest rate above the rate of return of the system is a cumulative disequilibrium, which finally explodes, and the economy collapses and ends up in a banking crisis. The problem is that utopianism decides the expansion of government expenditures, and monetary orthodoxy is the dogmatic rationalism which is tantamount to what I have called «the obscurantism of reason». This lethal symbiosis of «solidarity» and «dogmatic rationalism» has been at the center of the entire recent financial crisis. We have then to acknowledge that once you cannot control government expenditures neither you can control the nominal exchange rate and the money supply.

4. Ethics and Liberty

The history of mankind has been dramatic or even tragic. War was always the reason of states. In such a world ignorance and lack of information was the natural character of societies. So poverty, sloth and barbarism prevailed for more than five thousand years. The very idea of freedom was alien to humanity where work was slavery and trade was despicable until very recently. Our own world as perceived from the past could not be more than a utopia, however we seem to have a romantic perception while we disqualify the present in ethical terms.

It is this ethical approach to the past while pretending in a rousseunian way that: «Our souls have been corrupted in proportion as our sciences and arts have advanced toward perfection» hinders any possibility to understand the world we live in. Notwithstanding that romantic view of the past we are accepting an image of the so called Western Civilization as a coalition of Christian virtue and the reason of the Enlightenment. Consequently we are ignoring the deep ethical antagonism prevailing within our own Western society, regardless the antagonism with the Moslem world.

It was Karl Popper who in his essay:«The History of Our Time; An Optimist View» wrote: «I assert that our own free world is by far the best society which has come into existence during the course of human history»: There is no doubt that in spite of the present difficulties the world has improved since relatively recent time. But it is not only important to recognize the wonders of the present world, but it is even more important to understand the actual causes of this historical achievement.

The first thing that we have to recognize is that there was not a secular historical advance of the world. The history of mankind shows fairly clear that there was a turning point in time, and from then on the economy and the population started to grow. Let me remind the simple analysis of Simon Kuznets on this subject. In his «Modern Economic Growth» he wrote: «if per capita product had grown 15% per decade for three centuries before the 1960s, per capita product in the 1660s would have been 1//66th of the present level. But a per capita income at even a twenthieth of the present levels could not have sustained the population of even the most developed countries; and the assumed rates of growth in per capita product could not have been maintained in most countries for more than two centuries».

One hundred years before Karl Marx agreed with the above conclusion, and so he said in «The Communist Manifesto» :published in 1848 : «The bourgeoisie, during its rule of scarcely one hundred years, has created more massive and more colossal productive forces than have all preceding generations together». Hence we may conclude that economic growth or the perfection of arts and sciences did not start before 1750.

Evidently the causes which determined this advance were not economic as such, but economic growth was the consequence of deep changes in ethical and political ideas. We may say then that the so called Industrial Revolution, actually was a philosophical and ethical revolution, which took into account man frailty as the starting point to organize political society. If was John Locke who for the first time took into account man frailty as a precondition for the organization of goverment. So he said that monarchs were also men in order to limit the prerrogatives of the kings. He also stated that men had natural rights which were: life, liberty, property and the pursuance of happiness. It was on such assertions that took place The Glorious Revolution in England un 1688. Later on David Hume said, «it is impossible to change or correct anything material in our nature, the utmost that we can do our circumstances and situation». And that new circumstance was the political system of the Rule of Law. That is the limitation of political power and the protection of individual rigths.

Those principles were carried out even further by the Americans, sometime later and in that sense allow me to quote Ira Glasser in that respect who wrote: «The early Americans did indeed invent a new form of government. But they did more than that: they declared a new purpose for government. That new purpose was the protection of individual rights. No government had ever before been created primarily for that purpose. Before 1787, the role of government was assumed to be the enforcement of community consensus aimed at making citizen virtuous and moral». In other words Americans learnt Locke and Hume approach to human nature in order to organize government accordingly, under the Rule of Law.

Then with respect to individual rigths it is important to recognize the ethical meaning of the rigth to the pursuance of happiness. That rigth is the actual recognition that private interest are not contrary to general interest. That is why we consider that the concept of individual rigths is the opposite to human rigths. Human rigths are supposed to be that the people should have the rigth that government provides them the happiness. So it was in the United States where for the first time the written constitution, along with the role of the Justice Department, determined the limitation of political power and the respect for individual rigths.

My contention then , is that the Anglo American political philosophy is not the product of any particular religious belief or any race. If Webber theory respecting the protestant capitalist ethics were right, then the industrial revolution should have taken place originally in Germany which was the cradle of Protestantism, and not England, where the break up with the Pope had sexual and economic connotation rather than theological. It was not either the result of a racial component, because even after Anglicanism prevailed during the Tudors, Great Britain continued being a poor country, where there was no freedom.. David Hume in his History of England describes the situation in the following way: «The English in that age were so thoroughly subdued that like the Eastern slaves, they were inclined to admire those acts of violence and tyranny, that were exercised over themselves and at their own expense». And with respect to the Cronwel revolution he said :»England had never known a more severe and arbitrary government than was generally exercised by the patrons of liberty».

Most unfortunately I can say that the true antagonism

in the world is not cultural or religious, but ideological. Socialist values are accepted as such, both by religious beliefs as well as by the romantic rationalism. In order to understand the reality that we are facing in the world today, it is necessary to understand this historical ethical and philosophical antagonism, and to achieve that understanding has been and still is my quest.

Hence there is a great confusion in the world and even more in that part of the world that considers itself as representing the Western Civilization. This confusion arises in two realms: the semantics and the conceptual. The first of these confusions is the result of ignoring the ethical and the political philosophy antithesis between the Anglo-American philosophy and the Franco-German one. As Balint Vazzony once wrote, they are as different as day and night. That confusion arices from the Enlightment and the French Revolution. This fact has been recently recognized by Peter Drucker when he said: «It cannot be denied that the Enlightment and the French Revolution contributed to liberty in the XIX century. But its contribution was totally negative». Actually what he was saying is that totalitarianism was the result of the Enlightment and so he says: «There is a direct line from Rousseau up to Hitler, a line that incuded Robespierre, Marx and Stalin». And I would add Kant, Hegel Fiechte and Herder. More recently Jean François Revel in his last book «Last Exit to Utopia» agrees with that conception and says: «Totalitarianism is Europe great modern innovation, its gift to the political thought».

At the same time, that philosophical confusion to which I refer as the syncretism of Western philosophy, is the pretentious nirvana of democracy in the West. Conceptually, democracy may be divided in two antithetical systems: the rule of law and the majority rule. Majority rule is the opposite of the protection of individual rights. The apparent rights of the majorities is no more than the absolute power of governments in the name of the people, that is the new deity. That is in Aristotelian terms demagoguery and that is why democracy fail in Latin America, and so it was in Europe where Hitler and Mussolini represented majority rule at its most common name: reason of the state.

In that respect we should remenber Thomas Jefferson words: «An elective despotism was not the government we fought for». And James Madison added: « in a society under the form of which the stronger faction can ready unite and oppress the weaker anarchy may as truly be said to rein as in state of nature where the weaker individual is no secured against the violance of the stronger». In those words we have the asserted ethics of the Rule of Law which is that majority cannot violate the rigths of the minorities.

In Europe, since the times of Montesquieu and with the decided influence of Rousseau, democracy has been confused with socialism under the aegis of equality. Equality under the law is the opposite of that sort of equality which in socialism leads to the arbitrariness of government, which appear to be representing the ethics of the society against private interests. Unfortunately the left has monopolized the ethics of the society against the materialism of private interest. That is, the assumption that private interests are against the general interests becomes the excuse of socialism to violate the rule of law, that is the limit of political power.

The acceptance that democracy is the result of universal suffrage and capitalism the materialism of the private interest is the cause that the left has done what Rush Limbaugh have called «political cleansing» and monopolize the ethics of society in the name of equality. So the system of the rule of law had been called by Marx, capitalism. In that sense, the systems becomes the realm of materialism through the two Marxist approaches: the alienation and the theory of exploitation. Hence, the left appears to be the moral defensor of the people violating individual rights.

In the last years there has been an increasing concern in the United States for what is now known as the American exceptionalism. The relevant question then is what has been the cause of that exceptionalism. The answer to this question is trascendental because depending on it, it will be possible or not for other countries to achieve freedom. There are some theories, that pretend to explain the American exceptionalism as the result of the inheritance of British freedom. I am going to take into account Hume's history of England because I do believe that the United States owes to him the main philosophycal principles of the

American exceptionalism. So referring to the times of the Tudors he said: «The Brittish in that era were so subdued that like the Eastern slaves, they were inclined to admire the acts of violence and tyranny that was exercised over them and their cost». And continue: «If England had continued being as it was at the time of Elizabeth I, we would be as poor as the Bavarian Cost». And referring to the Cronwell revolution he said: «England had never known a more severe and more arbitrary government, than was generally excercised by patterns of liberty».

Last but not least he wrote about the ancient English society: «Such a state of society was very little advanced beyond the rude state of nature: violence universally prevailed, instead of general and equitable maxisms. The pretended liberty of the times was only an incapacity of submitting to government...» Sorry for the lenths of these quotations, but I consider them of the utmost importance in order to validate or not, the arguments of the authors concerning the origin of American exceptionalism. If in England in that era liberty prevailed, as the authors sustain, then which was the reason of the pilgrims to abandon their home country? We should also remember that during the Tudors and Stuarts kingdoms, there were in England the Court of the Star Chambre and the Court of High Commission which was to fulfill the role of the Inquisition. I can say then, that liberty started in England in 1688 with the Glorius Revolution, but that was very much later than the entrance of the Pilgrims in America. That was the time when the Stuarts were expelled the second time from the throne of England. It was then when for the first time Locke's liberal principles were applied- Hence given the fact that monarchs were also men it was necessary to limit the King's prerogatives and respect individual rights.

Now coming to the history of the United States, let us analyse the book of Catherine Drinker Bowen, «The Miracle of Philadelphia».. There the author explains the difficulties faced by the Founding Fathers in order to approve the Constitution of 1787, which actually changed the history of the world. In that respect she shows that the states were unwilling to form a national Government and: «it was more difficult to go from Boston to Philadelphia than going to London. Then she quotes John Adams, when he said: «that from the beginning I had seen more difficult from our attempts to govern ourselves than from all the fleets and armies of Europe». According to Peter Butler: «The interests of Southern and Eastern States were as different as the interest of Russia and Turkey». By the same token James Madison referred to the State legislatures in such terms that we could even think that he was talking about Latinamerican states. But then let us see what Hamilton thought as expressed in letter 15 of the Federalist: «We may indeed with propriety be said to have reached almost the last stage of the national humiliation. There is scarcelly any thing that can wound the pride or degrade the character of an independent nation, which we do not experience».

Let me say that it is not my purpose to disquality the American exceptionalism, but on the contrary to recognize the brilliance of the Founding Fathers for being able to create a country of freedom in that difficult environment. And then the American eceptionalism is not in the field of economic, but in the ethical and political order. It is in that sense that I cannot but to recognize the influence of David Hume on the Founding Fathers and mainly on James Madison. It is really surprising the present confusion in the United States between socialism and liberalism, as well as the apparent ignorance of the conservatives of the liberal principles which were philosophical pillars of the exceptional American political system.

It is evident that when Madison was writing letter 51 of The Federalist, he was taking into account and even paraphrasing Hume' s basic political thought. So Hume said: «It is only from the selfishness and confined generosity of men along with the scanty provision nature has made for his wants that justice derives its origin.... It is evident that the only cause why the extensive generosity of man, and the perfect abundance of everything, would destroy the very idea of justice, is because they render it useless». Then following Locke's principles of human nature Madison says: «But what is government itself but the greatest of all reflections or human nature. If men were angels no Government would be necessary». If angels were to govern men, neither external not internal controls on government would be necessary.» Then I may conclude that the American exceptionalism does not depend on his history, culture or religion, but on the liberal ideology recognized by the Founding Fathers, and stablished as the Rule of Law, that is the limitation of political power and the respect for the individuals rights: life, liberty, property and the pursuance of happiness.

5. The Rule of Law and True Democracy in the World

The political language of our world is full of words and absent concepts of governance. To understand the present chaotic political situation one must clarify the meaning of those words in terms of underlying ethical principles and their political implications in assuring individual rights in a true democracy.

The current ethical posturing of politicians, intellectuals and the media consists of protesting inequity in the distribution of wealth inside countries and between the industrial and underdeveloped world. The political argument then relates to ethical and not economic principles. It is apparent at the same time that concern for increasing poverty around the world fosters proposals to destroy the very economic system, which created real individual freedom , quality of life and prosperity for the first time in history .

Most unfortunately, this free enterprise system, which was denominated by Marx as Capitalism, is being ethically disqualified for inequity and the exploitation of workers,however defined. No one is standing up to defend our system in ethical terms, ignoring that so-called capitalism is not an economic system, but an ethical and political one. In essence, it is the defense of individual rights- Life ,Liberty, property and the right of men and women to pursue their own happiness, and the establishment of limitation of political power. Those are the essential principles of the Rule of Law, and the primary rule is that majorities do not have the right to violate the rights of minorities or individuals. It is the direct opposite of the « reason of the state» in the name of the people.

It is the same ethical misconception regarding capitalism presented by Lenin in his « Imperialism the Last Stage of Capitalism «. Hence, the United States appears as the evil empire, which exploits the rest of the world. That ethical approach suits the current domestic demagoguery of politicians around the world in their struggles for political power. Socialism, which was actually the name given by the Enlightenment to this demagoguery, is the ideology that prevails as the way to reach and maintain political power.

The current political environment is hardened by a great divide, between right and left. The right is becoming by definition ethically disqualified as representing the interests of the rich against the left, which pretends to represent the interest of the poor. As throughout history, the poor are always more than the rich and, as observed by Aristotle,, it is then obvious that Democracy in a country becomes the reign of majority rule and consequently confused with Socialism. As it was very well stated by Tocqueville, « Socialism and the concentration of power are fruits of the same soil». The consequence is more poverty in the absence of individual rights. And let us remember that when needs become rights, then governments violate the rights of the producers of wealth and products that may satisfy the needs.

Last and perhaps most important, in 1912 Von Misses wrote « the problem with socialism is that even those who oppose it accept its essential ethical premises». That is the situation we are facing today and why it is so important to tell the people of the wisdom of Thrasimacus when he said concerning the characteristics of man, « His psychological make up is simple: he is out to get what he wants, and what he wants is narrowly circumscribed. Power and pleasure are his exclusive interests. But to get what he wants this wolf has to wear the sheep's clothing of traditional moral values. His masquerade can only be carried through by putting the conventional moral vocabulary to the service of his private interest. He must say in the law courts and the assembly what the people want to hear, so they put power into his hands......He must take them by the ear before he takes them by the throat «

6. Liberalism and the Nation

The French Revolution significantly influenced the country's (Argentina) decision to severe political ties with Spain. The Enlightenment had already foreseen the possibility to establish an independent state in the territories that until 1816 had constituted the former Vice Royalty of the River Plate. Nevertheless, this endeavor resulted being more difficult than originally contemplated.

The destruction of Spain political authority in the Vice Royalty of the River Plate brought to the forefront profound contradictions that had until then been suppressed by the absolutist regime. The revolution was carried out under Buenos Aires' hegemony and influenced by the incorrect so-called Great Revolution.

The break of Spain from its onset heralded a modification of the internal regime with the resulting republic arising as an alternative to a domestic monarchy. With agreement on the constitution of the republic, the absolutist nature of the project brought to forefront with it an evident dispute between centralization and localism.

It goes without saying that the freedom of commerce that replaced the previous monopolistic system of the colonial period benefited directly the Province of Buenos Aires. This benefit nevertheless remained indirect and much less perceptible to the other provincial economies, many of which were truly subsistence economies.

No less important in this sense was the Province of Buenos Aires' declaration of religious freedom in 1825. As Alberdi argues, in the other provinces religious authoritarianism continued to reign governed by the *Laws of the*

Indies. This contradiction fuelled the apparent natural divergence between the Province of Buenos Aires and the others provinces. Similarly, as a result of being a free trade nation, there arose the problem of customs revenue distribution.

It was (Bernardino) Rivadavia who pursued the nationalization of those revenues. The first president's simplicity, as it pertained to the possibility of «Porteño» (Buenos Aires), led centralization emulating the enlightened despotism of the French Revolution, clashed with the local and «caudillo» idiosyncrasy of the provinces.

As Alberdi sustained, that «caudillismo» was present in the Province of Buenos Aires and personified by Juan Manuel de Rosas, who went on to recover the remnants of colonial principles which according to Alberdi were still in the hearts. Thus, federalism recognized the feudal schema that had characterized the *Laws of the Indies*.

The country integrated, or better disintegrated, into a type of confederation that on the surface remained answerable to Rosas, but whose fourteen internal customs regimes led to the Balkanization of the former Vice Royalty of the River Plate. Lost in the process were territories of Upper Peru (Bolivia), Paraguay, and Uruguay, largely as a consequence of the arbitrary nature of «porteño» politics, with the Indians ruling supreme in the south up through the Salado River region.
Consequently the cry of «religion or death» came to

characterize the de-evolution that the embryonic nation was submitted to at the hands of the «caudillos», who also lived by the rallying call of «death to the savage Unitarians».

Undoubtedly, neither Unitarianism nor Rosaism provided an adequate constitution for the republic. Thus with the following fall of Rosas, Argentina remained divided, underpopulated, poor and ignorant. This characterized the landscape of 1853, when Urquiza after defeating Rosas at the battle of Caseros, sought to implement from his stronghold in Paraná a constitution, which, as I have already indicated, predated those of continental Europe by nearly a century.

The possibility of organizing national unity has to traverse the convulsive 1853-1862 period. Once the constitutional amendments are ratified in 1860, general Bartolomé Mitre is inaugurated in Buenos Aires as the first president of the federal republic. This process would not have been possible without general Justo José de Urquiza's collaboration, who was nonetheless won over to the liberal cause by Alberdi's work and Domingo Faustino Sarmiento's perseverance.

The birth of the republic was the struggle for civilization, enthroned by the liberal principles included in the Constitution of 1853. Within this context, Mitre's decision to participate in the War of the Triple Alliance should be analysed.

It was president Mitre who saw that war with Paraguay was the symbol of his country's own internal ideological struggle. That is to say, the need to achieve politically the objectives of the nation's constitution. Without doubt, at the moment, Paraguay represented caudillismo's greatest threat to the recently born republic.

It was Alberdi who argued in «Las bases», that of South America's constitutions, Paraguay's was the worst. He stated, «The Oriental (Uruguay) constitution is the most advisable, whereas Paraguay's, the least». This represented a truly dangerous threat that jeopardized the integrity of the nation, since Solano López in Paraguay was representative of the sort of repression that had come to characterize the government of Rosas.

Nevertheless, the attitude that had until recently backed Rosas persisted in the provinces and was made clearly evident by the fact that Urquiza's own army resisted the call up to fight the Paraguayans. It seems that Urquiza's enlightenment had not permeated within his own province, leading to the distinct possibility that the Littoral and even possibly the province of Santa Fe would breakaway and merge with Paraguay.

The war of the Triple Alliance, in my judgement, set the stage from the Argentine perspective, for what can today be considered to be the nation's greatest ideological challenge threatening constitutional and national unity. A victorious Paraguay would have guaranteed the dismemberment of Argentina and subsequently a return to the

Laws of the Indies that had fallen from grace with the defeat of the «Restorer of Order» (Rosas).

Even though differences existed with the empire (Brazil), the same never represented a threat emanating from within society to the nation's integrity. Nor was the Oriental Shore (Uruguay), whose constitution was deemed by Alberdi to be the most advisable and similar to Argentina's, a threat.

Proof of this is that following the war, which marked a historical watershed in national unity under republicanism, Argentina surpassed Brazil by the end of the century, and its Gross Domestic Product (GDP) came to exceed that of all South America's combined. For its part, Uruguay from then onwards never constituted a threat to the liberal progress that had built the (Argentine) nation.

The Paraguayan challenge returned, and the nationalism with it, introduced again the principles that reigned in Paraguay and pretended to guide the country's independent development process. The view of Paraguay as an industrial power under the dictatorship of Solano López merits a summary analysis.

In that sense, I will cite the words of Jorge Thompson in *La Guerra del Paraguay*, and quoted by (doctor) Luis García Martínez in his brilliant exposition before the Academy of Economics, *The Root of the North-South Rupture*.

He states, «The majority of the population was the most content in the world. They minimally needed to work in order to gain their livelihoods. Each family had its own house or hut on its own land. They would sow in just a few days, and leave to its own devices until the next harvest, the tobacco, maize, and mandioca that they would need for personal consumption. Each hut had its own orange grove, whose fruit forms an important consumption item in Paraguay, and a few head of cattle, thus freeing a large portion of the population from the need of having to work». It is difficult to conceive a society whose regard par excellence of happiness was not to work, could constitute the paradigm of independent development.

7. The Exceptionalism of the United States

President Obama has brought fore an ideological antagonism, I would say for the first time in the history of the United States. Already in the XIX century the argentine Domingo Faustino Sarmiento wrote: «the Americans have agreed on everything that in the rest of the world has been the cause of opposition and revolutions». I may say that at that time Sarmiento had become aware about the American exceptionalism, what today seems to be in the United States the name of the game. I do believe that United States constitutes and has constituted an exception in history. It was also recognized by the also argentine Juan Bautista Alberdi, who wrote: «It is my conviction, that without the England and the United States, liberty would disappear in this century». The relevant question is: which has been the cause of that exceptionalism? The answer to this question is trascendental, because depending of the answer it will be possible or not for other countries to achieve their own freedom.

In *An Exceptional Debate*, a recent essay by Richard Lowry and Rammesh Ponnuru, the authors try to answer that question. In it they sustain that what the conservatives want to conserve may be reagarded as the pillars of American exceptionalism. According to the authors the American exceptionalism, was inherited from the English liberty. So they say: «English society thus had a more individualistic cast than the rest of Europe, which was centralized, hierarchical, and feudal by comparison». «The U.S. was the spawn of English liberalism, fated to carry it out to its logical conclusion and become the most liberal polity ever known to man». «American took inherited English liberty». So according to the above considerations, American exceptionalism started with the arrival of the pilgrims.

Let us start by analyzing the history of England, since it is from there that liberty came to America. I am going to take into account Hume's history of England because I do believe that the United States owes to him the main philosophycal principles of the American exceptionalism. Speaking about the times of the Tudors he says: «The Brittish in that era were so subdued that like the Eastern slaves, they were inclined to admire the acts of violence and tyranny that were exerted over them and their cost». And continues: «If England had continued being as it was at the time of Elizabeth I, we would be as poor as the Bavarian Court». And referring to the Cromwell revolution he says: «England had never known a more severe and more arbitrary government, than was generally exercised by the patrons of liberty».

Last but not least he wrote about the ancient English society: «Such a state of society was very little advanced beyond the rude state of nature: violence universally prevailed, instead of general and equitable maxims: The pretended liberty of the times was only an incapacity of submitting to government: And men, not protected by law in their lives and properties, sought shelter, by their personal servitude and attachments under some powerful chieftain, or by voluntary combinations....» I must apologize for the lengths of these quotations, but I regard them of utmost importance to validate the arguments of the authors concerning the origin of American exceptionalism. If in England in that era liberty prevailed, as the authors sustain, then which was the reason for the pilgrims to abandon their home country? We should also remember that during the Tudor and Stuart kingdoms, there were in England the Court of the Star –or Starred– Chamber and the Court of High Commission which were to fulfill the role of the Inquisition. It can be said then, that liberty started in England in 1688 with the Glorius Revolution, that is to say a long time after the voyage of the Pilgrims to America. That was the time when the Stuarts were expelled for the second time from the throne of England. It was then when for the first time Locke's liberal principles were applied: Hence given the fact that monarchs were also men it was necessary to limit the King's prerogatives and respect individual rights.

Now coming to the history of the United States, let us analyze the book of Catherine Drinker Bowen, «The Miracle of Philadelphia». In it the author explains the difficulties faced by the Founding Fathers in order to approve the Constitution of 1787, which actually changed the history of the world. In that respect she shows that the states were unwilling to form a national Government and: «it was more difficult to go from Boston to Philadelphia than going to London.» Then she quotes John Adams, as he said: «that from the beginning I had seen more difficult from our attempts to govern ourselves than from all the fleets and armies of Europe». According to Peter Butler: «The interests of Southern and Eastern States were as different as the interest of Russia and Turkey». By the same token James Madison referred to the State legislatures in such terms that we could even think that he was talking about Latin American states. But then let us see what Hamilton thought as expressed in letter 15 of the Federalist: «We may indeed with propriety be said to have reached almost the last stage of the national humiliation. There is scarcely anything that can wound the pride or degrade the character of an independent nation, which we do not experience».

Let me say that it is not my purpose to disqualify the American exceptionalism, but on the contrary to recognize the brightness of the Founding Fathers for being able to create a country of freedom in such a difficult environment. And the foundations of the American exceptionalism are not located in the field of economics, but in the ethical and political order. It is in that sense that I cannot but recognize the influence of David Hume over the Founding Fathers and mainly on James Madison. It is really surprising the present confusion in the United States between socialism and liberalism, as well as the apparent ignorance of the conservatives of the liberal principles that constitute the philosophical pillars of the exceptional American political system.

It is evident that when Madison was writing his letter 51 of *The Federalist*, he was taking into account and even paraphrasing Hume's basic political thought. So Hume said: «It is only from the selfishness and confined generosity of men along with the scanty provision nature has made for his wants that justice derives its origin ... It is evident that the only cause why the extensive generosity of man, and the perfect abundance of everything, would destroy the very idea of justice, is because they render it useless». Then following Locke's principles of human nature Madison says: «But what is government itself but the greatest of all reflections or human nature. If men were angels no Government would be necessary». «If angels were to govern men, neither external not internal controls on government would be necessary.» And on the same line Hume says: «They cannot change their nature. All they can do is to change their situation, and render the observance of justice the inmediate interest of some particular person and its violation their more remote». And that change of circumstances is the ethical and political system based on the rule of law, where as Madison clearly stated, the majorities do not have the right to violate the rights of minorities.

Then I may conclude that the American exceptionalism does not depend on his history, culture or religion, but on the liberal ideology recognized by the Founding Fathers, and stablished as the Rule of Law, that is the limitation of political power and the respect for the individuals rights: life, liberty, property and pressure of happiness. Let us hope that President Obama does not forget these pillars of the American exceptionalism.

II. Roman Law and the Rule of Law

1. Natural Law and Positive Law

According to Roscoe Pound, the alternative between Natural Law and Positive Law started at the time of the Greeks and was followed by the Roman law. So referring to the Romans, he says in his *Introduction to the Philosophy of Law*, «Hence what to the Greeks was a distinction between right of nature and right by convention or enactment became to them a distinction between law by nature and law by custom or legislation».

My contention is that the above alternative is not the important one. Before entering into the subject, I wish to remember Kant's dictum: *fiat iustitia, et pereat mundus* (do justice even though the world could perish). Coming back to my contention, this is a great fallacy, because the one and only end of justice is precisely to hinder the possibility that the world would perish.

Now then, the alternative between law of nature and what we call positive law is immaterial if we do not define what justice is and its purposes. And this distinction comes from the very nature of Roman law, and as Pound says,

«The jurisconsults were practical lawyers and the paramount interest in the general security was ever before their eyes... But the juristic empiricism by which the *ius civile* was made into law of the world needed something more than a theoretical incentive». The creation of the *ius civile* was more the empiricism of the *ius gentium* which was in charge of the «praetor peregrinus». And so Pound recognizes, «It was a process very like that by which Anglo-American judicial empiricism has been able to make a law of the world on the basis of the legal precepts of seventeenth century England».

In England of the seventeenth century, the idea of law was influenced by John Locke, who used the idea of natural law in order to justify his concept of individual rights. So in his letter concerning toleration, he wrote, «Civil interests I call Life, Liberty, Health and Indulgency of Body and the possession of outward things». Here we have the individual rights as such, which in his view are the natural rights. So much so that whether we agree or not (and I do not) with him in that very letter of toleration, he establishes that it is not possible to be tolerant with the atheist, because they do not respect the law of nature. Later on, Locke, in his *Second Treatise on Civil Government*, repeats the above sentence, but in a different way and considers that the law of nature provides the rights of men «to preserve their property, their life, their liberty and their Estate».

Pound however contends that there is a difference between the American and the British approach to natural law. So he says with respect to the American variant of natural law, «It was not that natural law expressed the nature of man. Rather it expresses the nature of governments». I certainly do not agree with this contention since in fact the nature of government as conceived by the Founding Fathers reflected precisely their conception with respect to the fallibility of man's nature.

It is precisely based on this assumption that Locke in his *Second Treatise* argues against absolute monarchy and so he says, «But I shall desire those who make this objection to remember that absolute monarchy are but men, and if Government is to be the remedy for those evils, which comes from men being judges in their own cases and the state of nature is therefore not to be endure... I desire to know what kind of government that is, and how much better it is than the state of nature, where one man commanding a multitude has the liberty to be judge in his own case, and may do to all his subjects whatever he pleases without the least liberty to anyone to question or control those who execute the pleasure». And then, in the chapter of Political or Civil Society, he adds the following reflection, «As if when men quitting the state of nature entered into society, they agreed that all of them but one should be under the restraint of Laws, but that he should retain all the liberty of the state of nature increased with power, and made licentious by Impunity. This is to think that men are so foolish that they take care to avoid what mischiefs may be done by polecats or foxes but are content may think it safety to be devoured by Lions».

The above quotations are the main arguments to limit political power although Locke did not include the separation of the judicial power as the main instrument to limit political power. Hence we can say that contrary to Pound's contention, the organization of the government was a reflection on human nature as it was to be clearly expressed by James Madison in Letter 10 of *The Federalist Papers*.

I would say, then, that natural rights are not the product of human nature, but in spite of it. And the way to comply with those rights was the limitation of political power or what he called «prerogatives». And for that purpose the role of the parliament was paramount. The problem was that as the king prerogatives were reduced, factually parliament took care of them.

It is true that in England prevailed the so-called common law, which reflected costume, and essentially the role of judges was to interpret and apply the law. Actually they created the law with a pragmatic approach to solve the problem in the name of equity. But we should not forget that at the time of Elizabeth there existed three Courts which actually were completely submitted to the political power. Those were the Court of the Star Chamber, the Court of the High Commission and the Martial Court. As regards the functions of those Courts, Eugene Miller said, «The Star Chamber possessed an unlimited discretionary authority to impose penalties for a variety of offences not covered by common law, and its members consisted of men who enjoyed the offices during the king's pleasure. The king himself was in fact the sole judge when he was present; the Court of the High Commission exercised jurisdiction over the crime of heresy; and martial law powers could be used to inflict swift punishment on the pretext of insurrection or public disorder».

In spite of this reality, Locke did not refer to the judicial power in his *Treatise*, though we should take into account that at the time he wrote it, the Court of the Star Chamber and the Court of High Commission had been already abolished. But before entering into the separation of the judicial power in the way prescribed by Montesquieu, I think advisable to delve into the concept of justice as conceived by David Hume.

Contrary to Locke, Hume's approach to justice and rights is completely alien to the concept of Natural Law, but is based precisely on human nature. So he says in his *Treatise on Human Nature*, «Here then is a proposition, which, I think, may be regarded as certain, that it is only from the selfishness and confined gerosity of men, along with the scanty provision nature has made for his wants, that justice derives its origin [...]. But it is evident that the only cause, why the extensive generosity of man, and the perfect abundance of every thing, would destroy the very idea of justice, is because they render it useless».

From the above quotation it is easily perceived that Hume's concept of justice is not a reflection of natural rights but it is based on the nature of man and the character of its natural surroundings. Hence he considers justice as an artificial virtue which is deeply related to the very nature of private property. In that sense, the main characteristic of property is that it is established by convention. Hence he distinguishes between moral and justice. Morality then is a natural virtue arising from the passions of men and in that sense it is opposed to the concept of rational morality as conceived from Plato's *Phaedo* to Kant's *Fundamental Principles of the Metaphysics of Morals*.

By the same token, morality is intentional whereas justice is consequential. And in that sense, we can say that this is a pragmatic approach to law as it was mainly the *ius gentium* and not the Justinian codification of the sixth century after Christ. At the same time, Hume does not consider that artificial means arbitrary but all the way around. And that is why he says, «Self-interest is the original motive to the establishment of justice; but sympathy with public interest is the cause of the moral approbation, which attends that virtue». So Hume determines, «The three fundamental laws of nature, that of stability of possession, the transference by consent and of the performance of promises. It is on the strict observance of those laws that the peace and security of human society entirely depend.

2. The Judiciary Power

We have already talked about justice, property and the limitations of political power, but we have not touched upon the necessary independence of the judiciary in order to be able to apply the law and recognize the limits of political power. That was originally the contribution of Charles Louis de Secondat, baron de La Brède et de Montesquieu. In his book *The Spirit of Laws*, he wrote, «There is no freedom if the power to judge is served from the legislative power. If it is not separated from the legislative, it would be possible to arbitrarily ignore the freedom and the life of the citizens; as the judge would be legislator. It is not separated from the executive power, the judge would have the power of an oppressor».

It is my understanding that from the above paragraph Montesquieu has been recognized as the originator of the theory of the separation of powers. In that sense, I would say that the contribution of Locke to that theory has been ignored, since as we explained above, he did not refer to the juridical power, for the reasons that we gave before.

I consider that this recognition has been a great historical mistake, because Montesquieu ignored the very reasons why it was necessary to establish the distribution of power. That is when he defines the conditions on which the Republic is based, he establishes the virtue of the citizens and then he says, «But political virtue is the unselfishness, the generosity, what is most difficult. It is possible to define this virtue saying that it is the love to the fatherland and to the laws. This love which always prefers the public good to its own generates all the private virtues which compound those preferences». And he continues, «The love to the Republic in a democracy is the love to equality. By giving all the same well-being and the same advantages, they should enjoy the same pleasures and to have the same hope. That is not possible if frugality is not general».

We can see from the above quotation that Montesquieu in the eighteenth century was already looking for the good savage (Rousseau) and the new man (Marx). Hence, he ignores the very reason of liberty and of course of private interests and, as a consequence, of individual rights.

3. Ius Gentium and Codification

Now that we have already analyzed the instrument as well as the essence of the reason from the separation of powers, we should continue our argument with respect to the difference between the original law creation through the ius gentium in Rome, as it was inherited by the Anglo-American common law, and the Justinian codification, which influenced the Continental juridical system. In this respect, Hayek in *The Constitution of Liberty*, wrote, «The famous Laws of the Twelve Tables reputedly drawn up in conscious imitation of Solon's laws from the foundation of its liberty. The first public laws in them provides «that no privilege or statues shall be enacted in favour of private persons, to the injury of others contrary to the law common to all citizens, and which individuals no matter of what rank have a right to make use of». This was the basic conception under which it was gradually formed, by a process very similar to that by which the common law grew, the first fully developed system of private law —in spirit very different from the later Justinian Code, which determined the legal thinking of the Continent».

According to Hayek, it was Cicero who developed the concept of freedom under the law. That is, that there is no conflict between law and freedom. This concept was also established by John Locke in his *Second Treatise on Civil*

Government, where he said that there is no freedom without law. This concept was even more extended by David Hume and in this respect Eugene F. Miller in his essay «Hume on the Development of English Freedom» says, «True liberty, as Hume understands it, incorporates the restraint of law. It requires such limitations as are necessary to make the individual secure from harm, whether from other individually or from government». So he insists that the freedom of individual can be limited only by laws and not by a prerogative or discretionary power in the executive». And Miller continues, «What Hume fears is not so much the tyranny of the people as the tyranny of popular assemblies dominated by leaders who claim to speak for the people. Popular assemblies are by their size, exempt in great measure from the restraint of shame and when they overleap the bounds of law, they naturally break out into acts the greatest tyranny and injustice».

We can see that these principles were the ones which were later developed in the United States to establish the rule of law as the antithesis of the reason of state prevailing in the continent which is philosophically based on the reality of the universals, like the state, the nation, the people, etcetera, and is the very expression of the absolute prerogatives of the political power. This is to ignore the «surprising» finding of Locke, when he discovered the fact that monarchs were also men.

It is in this respect that Miller recognizes the difference between British and the continental philosophy of history and so he says, «Hume subordinates the study of history to moral science, the fundamental premise of which is that human nature is constant and uniform. Indeed, the chief use of history «is only to discover the constant and universal principles of human nature, by showing men in all varieties of circumstances and situations, and furnishing us with materials from which we may form our observations and become acquainted with the regular springs of human action and behavior»».

«Continental philosophy of history, by contrast, would proceed on the assumption that human beings have no fixed nature. In order to understand man, we must study his development; and history is the field in which this development occurs. The aim or end of human development is freedom, and history moves inexorably towards the full realization of this end.» This Hegel approach following Kant's reason in history was later superseded by Marx end of history in the classless society.

So there is a great difference between accepting that there is no freedom without law (Locke) and the pretension that all freedom is the result of law (Hegel). That is the difference between liberty and oppression. In the first case, everything that is not forbidden is permitted whereas the second one means that only those things that are legally permitted are not forbidden.

But coming back to the origins of the rule of law, let us see what Hayek says in this respect. And he says, «During the later empire, the strict law was weakened as, in the interest of a new social policy, the state increased its control over economic life. The outcome of this process, which culminated under Constantine, was, in the words of a distinguished student of Roman law, that «the absolute empire proclaimed together with the principle of equity the authority of the empirical will unfettered by the barrier of law. Justinian with his learned professors brought this process to its conclusions». Thereafter, for a thousand years, the conception of legislation that should serve to protect the freedom of the individual was lost. And when the art of legislation was rediscovered, it was the code of Justinian with its conception of a prince who stood above the law that served as the model in the Continent».

From the above quotation we may accept this thesis which states that the real inheritors of Roman law were the Anglo-Americans. On the other hand, continental Europe and obviously Latin America inherited the Codification and with it the notion that the political power is above the Law. That is one of the main reasons why democracy failed in Europe and it is showing again its weakness under the aegis of social democracy. Needless to say, that in Latin America during the last thirty years «universal suffrage» has been just the excuse to violate individual rights by law.

4. The American Legal System

The greatest contribution of the Americans to political philosophy was the institution of the written Constitution and the fundamental role of the Supreme Court as the guardian of the Constitution. In letter 78 of *The Federalist*, Hamilton wrote in this respect, «No legislative act therefore contrary to the Constitution can be valid. To deny this would be to affirm that the deputy is greater than his principal... A Constitution is in fact and must be regarded by the judges as a fundamental law. Therefore it belongs to them to ascertain its meaning as well as the meaning of any particular act proceeding from the legislative body».

The above principle was applied in 1803 by Judge Marshall in the famous case Madison vs. Marbury, where the Court stated, «All those who have framed written constitutions contemplate them as forming the fundamental and paramount law of the nation, and consequently the theory of every such government must be, that an act of the legislature, repugnant to the constitution, is void». «It is, emphatically, the province and duty of judicial department to say what the law is. Those who apply the rule to particular cases must of necessity expound and interpret the rule. If two laws conflict with each other, the courts must decide on the operation of each... If the courts are to regard the constitution, and the constitution is superior to any ordinary act of the legislature, the constitution, and not such ordinary act, must govern the case to which they both apply.»

This is the operating concept of the judicial review, which is the instrument by which political power can be checked. Obviously the underlying idea to explicitly control the government is the principle established by Madison in letter 51 of *The Federalist* and which reflects the wisdom of John Locke and David Hume in their respective concepts of the nature of government and the role of justice, considering the nature of man. Then Madison said, «But what is government itself but the greatest of all reflections on human nature? If men were angels, no government would be necessary. If angels were to govern men, neither external nor internal controls on government would be necessary. In framing a government which is to be administrated by men over men, the great difficulty lies in this: You must first enable the government to control the governed; and in the next place, oblige it to control itself. A dependence on the people is no doubt the primary control on the government; but experience has taught mankind the necessity of auxiliary precautions». Needless to say that above all, this role of the Supreme Court can be performed as long as it is independent from the political power.

I would say then that the American Constitutional System implies not only the formality of the separation of the state powers (limits to political power), but the juridization of philosophical principles included in the Bill of Rights (Constitutional amendments). Those rights may be accepted as the expression of natural rights (Locke) or as the result of a learning process about human nature (Hume). Hence the rule of law implies social agreement with respect to individual rights. That is why in the United States political discussions are always about issues within the province of the Constitution. That is the wisdom of the Republic which is completely different from the concept of majority rule, which is the democratic process in the rest of the world. So the system or the individual rights, life, liberty, property and the pursuance of happiness are never at stake or at least should never be at stake in the political arena.

Most important of the recognition is the recognition as well of the ethic of private interests, which are not opposed *per se* to the general interests. So much so that the right to the pursuance of happiness is the recognition of the ethic of private interest in this world as well as in the next. And in that sense, the words of Madison in letter 51 of *The Federalist* are more illuminating in this respect when he says, «In a free government, the security for civil rights must be the same as for religious rights. In the first case, it consists of the multiplicity of interests, and in the other, of the multiplicity of sects».

III. Syndicalism and Individual Rights

1. Types of Syndicalism

When dealing with the problem of syndicates, it is necessary to start by analyzing the character of the societies in which they develop and the values on which they are established. There are two different conceptions depending on the relationship between the concept of justice and the concept of private property. While in the democratic capitalist society private property is the origin itself of justice, in the totalitarian socialist society private property is the cause of injustice. The nature of syndicates as well as their functions is of a very different kind in each of these societies. In the first one, syndicalism has the purpose of guaranteeing the private interests of workers while in the second one it is a vertical structure that vertebrates the politic power of the State.

Likewise, in capitalist societies two types of syndicates of complete different nature have emerged. In some cases, the syndicate continues to be an instrument of the workers for the improvement of their working conditions within the limits pre-established by property rights; in the other, the purpose itself of syndicalism is the transformation of society and therefore, its conception and its operative are eminently of a political character even though its demands could seem economical.

2. The Rights of Association in Argentina

In Argentina, the political Constitution of 1853 guarantees both the right to property and the right of association. These rights are recognized in Article 14, which reads:
> «All inhabitants of the Nation enjoy the following rights, in accordance with the laws that regulate their exercise, namely: of working and practicing any lawful industry; of navigating and trading; of petitioning the authorities; of entering, remaining in, travelling through and leaving the Argentine territory; of publishing their ideas through the press without prior censorship; of using and disposing of their property; of associating for useful purposes; of freely practicing their religion; of teaching and learning».

The right to property is guaranteed in its most ample expression in Article 17, which reads:
> «Property is inviolable, and no inhabitant of the Nation can be deprived thereof except by virtue of a judgement supported by law.»

From the conjugation of these two articles emerges the need for labor associations to be submitted to the same principles as those established in the Wagner Act to which we will refer to later. In this way, syndicates are unable to limit the freedom to work nor threaten nor withhold the freedom of trade. Much less so could they have political ends since the freedom of association referred to in Article 14 expressly refers to useful purposes. Political strikes are an aggression to the stability of the government, which is, in turn, a fundamental presumption of the constitutional rights because it is itself responsible for defending them through the respective powers.

In this sense, Alberdi, in his *Economical and Financial System of the Argentine Confederation*, says, «But it was not enough to recognize property as an inviolable right. It can be respected in its principle and disregarded and attacked in what is most precious of it: in the use and availability of its advantages. Tyrants have more than once used this sophistic distinction to seize property that they did not dare to disown. The hypocrite and timid socialism which has not dared to deny the right to property has used the same sophism, attacking the use and availability of property in the name of the labor organization. Having this on sight, the Argentine Constitution has established by its Article 14 the full right to use and dispose of property with which it has put an iron lock to the advances of socialism».

Alberdi was not only worried about property, he was also worried about the right to free work. Based on Article 15, which prohibits the possession of slaves in Argentina, and Article 16, which establishes equality before the law and the inadmissibility of prerogatives of blood or birth, Alberdi develops his thesis on the rights that the Constitution offers to free work as the only source of wealth, where he repeats Locke in his *Second Treatise* about civil government. It was liberalism that laid the foundations of property in work, giving it, for the first time in history, the noble rank that it should acquire in the civil and democratic society. Alberdi says, «Elevating the slave to the level of a free man, the Constitution serves production powerfully because it prevents the disastrous concurrence between the free worker who works for himself and the slave worker who produces for his master; and it rehabilitates and dignifies work, degraded in hands of the slave turning it shameful to the eyes of the free man. Ennobling, glorifying labor by this means the Constitution places the citizen on the way to its true personal independence and freedom, since labor is the source of wealth by which means man shakes all servile I and constitutes himself as his true own master».

In this way, the Constitution protects labor and property and only requires suitability for the first one. That is, as a source of wealth, labor is only productive when it is competent and therefore, everything that restricts this competence contributes to reduce the efficiency of the system to produce wealth. Wages are, at first instance, the first affected by the inefficiency of the economic system and the worker ceases to be free not only due to his recurrent poverty but he passes on to be dependant in his miserable life of the political power that grants him the right to be unsuitable, that is, the right to live without working. The worker in these conditions has sold his birthright for a mess of pottage, changing work in freedom for the right to live miserably.

This indissoluble relationship between freedom, property and labor as a fundamental principle of the Constitution is acknowledged by Alberdi when he says, «We see by what we said before that the freedom considered in the Constitution has its effects and relationships with the economical production; it is both the principle of public and private wealth and a condition for moral welfare. Any law, according to this, any decree, any act that somehow restricts or compromises the principle of freedom is an attack, more or less serious, to the wealth of the citizen, to the Treasury of the State and to the material progress of the country. Despotism and tyranny, be they of power, of laws, or of regulations, annihilate in its origin the source of wealth, which is free labor, and are the cause of misery and shortage for the country and the origin of all the degradations that come along with poverty».

«By what has been said before it is clear that syndicate rights are doubly limited in the constitutional text. First, because they have to respect private property and second, because they cannot restrict in any way the freedom of labor, which is the condition of competence established by Article 16.» And thus, Alberdi continues saying, «Any regulation that under the pretext of organizing economic freedom in practice restricts it or embarrasses it commits a double transgression against the Constitution, which has in this freedom its most fertile principle. The right to work and to exercise any lawful industry is a freedom that embraces all the means of human production, with the only exception of illegal or criminal industry, this is to say, the industry which constitutes an attempt on the liberty of another and on the rights of a third. All the great school of Adam Smith comes down to demonstrate that free labor is the essential principle of all created wealth».

3. Syndicalism in the United States of America

There is no doubt that American syndicalism configures the character par excellence of the role that it has to play in a capitalist society, where property is respected. There, after a few years of fighting, the Supreme Court acknowledged the right that establishes the right to freedom of expression. The First Constitutional Amendment states:

«Congress shall make no law respecting an establishment of religion, or prohibiting the free exercise thereof, or abridging the freedom of speech, or of the press; or the right of the people peaceably to assemble, and to petition the Government for a redress of grievances.»

In 1935, the National Labor Relations Act (The Wagner Act) was enacted, and in its Section 1, «General Provisions», it states the following:

> «The inequality of bargaining power between employees who do not possess full freedom of association or actual liberty of contract, and employers who are organized in the corporate or other forms of ownership association substantially burdens and affects the flow of commerce, and tends to aggravate recurrent business depressions, by depressing wage rates and the purchasing power of wage earners in industry and by preventing the

stabilization of competitive wage rates and working conditions within and between industries.»
«Experience has proved that protection by law of the right of employees to organize and bargain collectively safeguards commerce from injury, impairment, or interruption, and promotes the flow of commerce by removing certain recognized sources of industrial strife and unrest, by encouraging practices fundamental to the friendly adjustment of industrial disputes arising out of differences as to wages, hours, or other working conditions, and by restoring equality of bargaining power between employers and employees.»
«Experience has further demonstrated that certain practices by some labor organizations, their officers, and members have the intent or the necessary effect of burdening or obstructing commerce. The elimination of such practices is a necessary condition to the assurance of the rights herein guaranteed.»

From the paragraphs of The Wagner Act transcribed above emerge the fundamental principles that rule syndicate rights in a democratic capitalist society. These were that the right of association acknowledged in the First Constitutional Amendment should be applied to the organization of syndicates, with the purpose of equalizing the power that such a right had in its objective of maintaining the free flow of commerce, which is undoubtedly the guarantee for property and particular interests. Finally, it is made clear that syndicate practises that tend to prevent this flow of commerce would be left aside of the rights acknowledged by law. This last principle means that syndicalism is legally framed by the norms that rule a society where property rights are guaranteed and therefore, those syndicate movements that have political purposes of transformation of the republican system of government that rules such a society are not protected by law.

4. Socialism, Communism and Syndicates

There is no doubt that communist and socialist syndicates do not fulfill the requirements that the Constitution establishes for property rights and for free labor. In other words, both one and the other attempt against the political system guaranteed by the Constitution. Such syndicates, far from being an instrument for the reinforcement of the system, constitute the political ram that tends to its destruction. Once the political system is destroyed, the same proletariat dictatorship prescribed by Marxism constitutes itself in the very element for the destruction of free labor, as the history of the communist societies has demonstrated where syndicate leaders are turned into the representatives of the political power to impose the obedience of the workers.

If there is any doubt left regarding the violence that Marxism implies with respect to the constitutional principles, it would be enough to read *The Communist Manifesto*, in its Chapter II: «Proletarians and Communists», where it says, «The immediate purpose of communists is the same as that of all other proletarian parties: the formation of proletarians in one class, the destruction of the supremacy of the bourgeoisie, and the conquest of power by proletarians».

It is evident that such objectives are not compatible with the Argentine Constitution and, particularly, with the freedom of commerce that it guarantees. Those objectives of the communist movement are sustained on the principle of the strife between classes, that is, the antagonism that arises between private property and workers. This antagonism, which in Marxist terms would reflect opposed interests between the property owner bourgeoisie and the proletariat class, results from the conception of the theories of alienation and of exploitation. According to these theories, the capitalist system deprives the worker of his personality and of the product of his work respectively. Taken these conditions for granted, in Marxism there is no possibility whatsoever of making the interests of both classes compatible and, therefore, its explicit commitment is the destruction of the bourgeoisie which is confused in the Marxist lexicon with the proprietary class by the proletarian class represented by the dictatorship of the proletariat. In this cosmovision, syndicates are nothing else than the instrument for political power as made explicit in *The Communist Manifesto*.

Syndicate freedom for syndicates with such objectives means nothing else than the freedom to destroy the system guaranteed by the National Constitution. But at the same time, it must be pointed out that they are based upon and are coherent with a vision of reality according to which freedom, in the constitutional sense, is contrary to the interests of workers, and also contrary to the national interests immersed in the international capitalist system. This position was later made more explicit by Lenin in his *Imperialism: Superior Stage of Capitalism,* where the theory of dependence is established, whereby surplus or increased value (result of exploitation) is transferred to countries that export capital. But it must not be forgotten that no theory of dependence exists if the Marxist-Leninist postulates of the theory of exploitation and its consequent transference by means of investment of foreign capital were not accepted.

5. Syndicalism and «Justicialismo»

Since 1946, syndicalism in Argentina has been taking a course that puts it every time further away from the principles established in the National Constitution. This new course arises precisely from a conception that disqualifies the capitalist system as representative of property rights and free labor. The preliminary principle of the socioeconomic transformation performed by the «Justicialismo» lies on sustaining that capital must be at the service of economy and not that economy should be at the service of capital. The profound State intervention in economy and the consequent role to be played by syndicates under this conception were based on this supposed ethical revision. The ethical principle was, in turn, complemented with an economic theory that was made explicit as the rupture from what dominated the Hedonic principle of capitalism. This was nothing else than the microeconomic theory of the optimum, represented by that level of production that equals marginal costs to marginal income. This economic theory of demand, which transcends even the Keynesian scheme and turns it into a theory of development in a different ethical outline, ignores in the best Marxist style the reality of shortage as a conditioning factor for economic chores. But what is important in what we are dealing with is not to demonstrate that this theory is invalid, but to show the outcome of this ethical–economic conception in terms of relationships between the State, the employers and the employees.

The paragraph previously cited shows clearly the absolute politization of the economic system whereby the State moves on to play a decisive role. The increases in wages are determined by the Government and, in this regard, it could be said that syndicates are submitted to political power. The impact of these increases in wages on the economics of business is a matter not to be discussed by employers, since they will have to increase production, whether they like it or not, in order to satisfy the demands. The problem is that shortage, ignored in the previous analysis, forces an increase in prices. The financing of this increase in prices, in order to avoid the collapse of the economic system, is the resource that remains in hands of the Government through the Central Bank, to impose the submission of employers to political power. Inflation is the only answer that the economic system provides to the ignorance of political power of the principle of shortage, arbitrarily named: The Hedonic Principle of Capitalism.

In this plan, we see the value of the generous intention of the government to increase worker incomes and once again, the managerial egotism, responsible for the increase in prices, appears. Of course, in the economic sphere, all notions of cost are lost and, therefore, the concept of efficiency of the economic system disappears. According to the theory of the present Minister of Planning, as he presents it in his book, *From the Culture of Income to the Economics of Production*, the «Justicialista» principle is directly responsible for such an operation and for the confirmation of this so-called *Culture of Income*.

The resulting system is necessarily a structure dependent on political power that contributes to impose on workers the decisions made by the Government. The Peronist party and the syndical movement thus join in this «justicialista» embrace that supposedly has the purpose of submitting capital to the demands of economy. The employer then gets trapped in the spider-web of political power, both in the entirely economic field and the ethical one. In the economic field, because he lacks the force to oppose himself to the wage demands that are decided from Government and exposed by syndicate leaders, evident employees of the political power and not real representatives of the workers. It does not really matter much to them since their economic survival is also guaranteed to them as long as it is equally submitted to political power, through the financing of the Central Bank. Inflation will restore the balance between real wages and the profits of capital. However, on ethical grounds he is still disqualified since he is the one who appears responsible for the loss of purchasing power of wages generally granted by political power.

It is evident that the previous plan means an obvious violation of constitutional principles that expressly guarantee private property and free labor. The system, notwithstanding its productive inefficiency, is relatively operative to the extent that syndicate power is absolutely submitted to political power, which is cautious enough not to distort the principle of shortage more than within certain limits. On the very same moment when political power loses control over syndicate power, and this one turns into a power itself, the economic system tends to break apart due to the rupture of the political system.

The syndical system turned into an autonomous power, and with a substantial financing through social security services imposes efficiency restrictions to the economic system which are precisely the ones that prevent that the wage levels demanded may be satisfied. The employers, of course, and notwithstanding the corporations that bind them together, are less observant of the real strife for power that takes place between the Government and the syndicates. To talk about collective conventions of work and of joint committees under such conditions is no more than a fallacy of labor culture. The democratic system is absolutely impracticable when the Government must face a syndical structure that has power but lacks any type of responsibility for the operative of the society as a whole.

The permanence of the *status quo* conceived as acquired rights (social conquests) and that guarantees the power of syndical leaders is reverted against the real wage of the worker. In other words, the demands for power of syndicate leaders are confronted indirectly, but evidently, to the interests of workers. Economy weakens and as the level of income decreases, more is the struggle for it; the risk of capital retraction increases and, as investment decreases, economy ceases to grow.

The political, economic and social plan described previously is the one that is reflected in the successive labor laws that started to be passed as from 1946. It is this plan that needs to be modified substantially to frame it within the constitutional principles of freedom to work and of guarantees to property rights. Never as in the last 40 years has the inconsistency of the ethical–economic movement that gave place to the syndical Argentine structure, nor, at the same time, the political–economic need to modify it, been more evident. It is precisely in the sense of the new conception of social justice, as expressed by the President in his speech before this Honourable Congress, that this bill for the modification of the Argentine Labor System is presented.

6. The Legislation in Force and its Antecedents in the Light of the Constitutional Principles

Even the slightest analysis of the labor legislation in Argentina since 1946 to our days shows an obvious violation of the constitutional principles. In this sense, and perhaps never again as in this case, has the situation so dreaded by Alberdi, regarding whether the Constitution could be violated under the pretext of protecting freedom, turned out to be true.

In Argentina, this reality was made more obvious when Article 14 (Bis) was introduced into its Constitution. Although this does not represent a modification *per se* of the principles established by the Constitution, a way has been opened that, in fact, allows that the concepts of syndical freedom contained in successive syndical laws represent a violation to property rights on the one hand and to freedom of work on the other.

The acknowledgement of union personality in all these laws to all those so-called «Third Grade Organizations» and the establishment of a unique syndicate are in contradiction with the syndical freedom pretended to be protected. Through the system of social security services the syndical movement has not only obtained a bountiful mechanism of financing but it also results as an *ad hoc* instrument to achieve compulsory affiliation.

It must be remembered that in Peron's times this activity was part of the duties of the Secretary of Labor and Social Prevision. That is, it was evident that syndicalists were not only controlled by the political power but also through the financing of their activities. Once Perón disappeared from the scene, the syndical movement thus constituted, and as described in the previous paragraph, inherited the hegemonic character that had been granted by its own constitution as well as the substantial incomes that the monopoly of social welfare services represented.

The system of homologation, establishing the limits of work contacts, represents likewise a restriction to property rights that, at the same time, restricts the freedom of workers.

These considerations regarding the totalitarian character of labor laws and the absence of true syndical liberty in Argentina were admitted in the report of the ILO (International Labour Organization) mission carried out in May, 1984. The report, which was sent to the Ministry of Work during the International Labour Conference in Geneva, points out the following general conclusions:

«Before making references in detail to the conclusions, certain general observations should be pointed out.»

«The first one refers to the historical moment in which this mission was situated. After several years, the Republic of Argentina has returned to a democratic regime, an evolution that cannot be sufficiently underlined, both with respect to the country itself and to all the American continent. It is normal that the freedom which has been installed in the political frame will extend also to syndical institutions, and ILO cannot but lend its entire assistance to such a type of evolution.»

«The second observation is that, for several years now, Argentine legislation and practice in syndicate matters were being subjects of periodical comments and discussions in the bosom of different organisms of ILO, and this much more so since the Argentine Republic has ratified the Agreement on syndicate freedom and the protection to the right of syndication, 1978 (Number 87). It would be very desirable that the new syndicate law would allow the incompatibilities that have existed between the legislation and this Agreement do dissipate, together with the consequent difficulties that have been periodically found in the bosom of ILO. In this way, the Argentine Republic could participate in the future in the activities of ILO with an increased prestige as a consequence of placing legislation in conformity with international commitments.

Apart from that and beyond the question of conformity with international rules, the establishment of a regime of true syndicate freedom and the constitution of representative and responsible syndicates would, no doubt, contribute to facilitate the internal evolution of the country and allow the set-up of a constructive social dialogue between the Government, the employers and the workers, in a period that is foreseen to be difficult from the point of view of economic problems.»

The report in question acknowledges, in most of its extension, the constitutional principles exposed above. To make a final point, the following expression in the report should be brought to our attention:

«The only legal dispositions compatible with syndicate freedom are, as indicated above, those related to the democratic performance of syndicates».

IV. Foreign Policy

1. Western Ethics and the Environment

I came here not to bury the Anglo-Saxons but to praise them. And I came to praise them because I really think that they invented the world we live in, through the influence of the English and Scottish philosophers and more than this because these ideas crossed the Atlantic and created this fabulous society that is the United States of America. I know that it is difficult for the Latin Americans to understand British philosophy because we have been influenced by another side of the thought. I really think that there is confusion in the world. Confusion that was created by thinking that there is something like the West, and I have my doubts; so many doubts that I wrote a book about it, asking *Who Is the West?* And I think that way because I have heard here that the world started to improve after the Enlightenment, but I can say that at the time we had the Enlightenment, we also had the «endarkment». I do not know if that word exists, but I hope it will be understood. Because in fact, I am not going to speak about environment because I only speak about things that

I do not know that I do not know. But I think that the problem of environment can be framed into the problem of ethics and that is what we have been arguing for more than hundred years. The Enlightenment had its first green in Rousseau. Jean Jack was the first green that I had ever heard about. Rousseau had an influence in the continent, and unfortunately as Latin America is a kind of farce of what the Europeans are, they influenced us very much and we confused that great advance of society that was the Glorious Revolution and the American Revolution with the French Revolution. That is unforgivable and we have paid dearly for this confusion.

What you may have called the Anglo-Saxon philosophy is based on four major rights: the right to life, the right to freedom and the right to property and more than that, the right of men to the pursuance of their own happiness. In my view, this last one is the most important ethical command. Why? Because that allows men to have private interest without thinking that they are sinners for that. So I think that that is the real liberalism. Unfortunately, Americans who sometimes make mistakes had confused this word, but now I have heard that some Americans call it «classic liberalism», like Coca-Cola classic. And on the other side, we have the opponents, who called it «neo-liberalism». But there is not such a thing as classic or neo-liberalism. There is something that is the ethical approach of liberalism that changed the world into whether we like it or not, it is what we somehow prefer although sometimes we deride all these values that really created the world we live in, that we like to live in. I think that it is important to know that Kant was the one who destroyed the Anglo-Saxon philosophy in the continent, and we inherited that. As the categorical imperative and the idea that we can know the phenomenon but not the noumenon, we thought that reason is everything and reason is just part of the game. Because I learnt from the Anglo-Saxon that men also have passions. And passions are the things that really direct our behavior sometimes influenced by reason. So we learnt from the Anglo-Saxon not rationality but what I would say to be reasonable, to know the limits of our possibilities as men, because we are fallible. Reason is a tool that we have but we can never confuse it with truth. Unfortunately, when people made mistakes, we used to say, «He is an irrational». The mistakes are all rational and they are still mistakes. Many intelligent people made the greatest mistakes; they had the opportunity to.

So I want to mention the one I consider the greatest philosopher in this era, he was David Hume. And I am going to say why. Because he realized that the origin of all knowledge is the knowledge of how the mind of the people operates. And what were the incentives and how people operate with the human nature. He tried to get the institution that was possible according to our mediocrity, if you want to put it in that way. Mediocrity is not a good word, but it is what we all are. And I want to quote him. He said this in his book *A Treatise on Human Nature*, which I really recommend you to read, if by any chance some of you had never read it, especially the part concerning morals, because, in fact, while we are discussing the problem of environment we are discussing morals or ethical values. And he said, «In general it may be affirmed that there is not such a passion in human mind as the love of mankind merely as such independent of personal qualities of services or of relations to ourselves. It is true that there is no human and indeed no sensible creature whose happiness or misery does not in some measure affect us when brought near to us and represented in lively colors but these proceeds merely from sympathy and it is not proved of such an universal affection to mankind since this concern extent itself beyond our own species». I think this is very remarkable. And it is more remarkable because in fact we are fighting the people who think that they love mankind and that we are the mankind haters. In fact, this idea of creating this sort of universal feeling out of this personal feeling that we all have some time or another is just a rationalization that creates oppression and gives the idea that we are what we are not. And that is why I remember that at some point James Madison... I think that James Madison was the creator of this society. I have a great admiration for him. He wrote something like if men were angels, we would not need government and if men were going to be governed by angels, we would not need to have any control on the government. I think he was really very influenced by David Hume, who had also said that justice was necessary. Let me quote him, «It is only from the selfishness and confined generosity of man along with the scanty provision that has made for his once that justice derives his origin». The origin of justice explains that property. The same artifice gives rise to both. That is the difference between moral and values and justice. And he thought that morality was a problem of feelings. Whereas Kant and the continent thought that there was a kind of morality that according to the categorical imperative everybody could know what the morality was and how we should behave in any instance. Unfortunately, Kant had a very strong influence in our thoughts, and we believe, like Alberdi, that the private thief is the least danger that private property faces. Thank you very much.

2. Intellectuals and Globalization

Since the crumbling of the Berlin Wall, a new theory has been developed, according to which the world advances in one direction of progress through liberal democracy. Capitalism efficiency, technology and communications predict the famous global village as if another historical mechanism would propel the world towards another Alfa together with the Solar system. So great has been the enthusiasm in this respect that a new oracle, Mr Fukuyama, predicted the end of history as a consequence of the disappearance of ideological antagonisms.

Let us remember that in the seventies another augur, this time a Polish-American Mr Zbigniew Brzezinsky, wrote another famous book, *Between Two Ages: America's Role in the Technetronic Era,* in which he had predicted a closer relationship between the United States and the Soviet Union as a consequence of technological development. So he wrote, «Technological developments make it certain that modern society will require more and more planning.

Deliberate management of the American future will become widespread with the planner displacing the lawyer as the key social legislator and manipulator». After the resounding crumbling of the Soviet Union, our oracle felt compelled to write another book: *The Great Failure*, which is the opposite view.

More recently, another product of Harvard, Mr Samuel Huntington, illuminated us with a new book in which far from sharing optimistic views and the idyllic perception respecting the Global Village, of his predecessors, he predicts a future world of multiple antagonisms. In his already famous *The Clash of Civilizations*, the new oracle predicts the replacement of the ideologies by his concept of civilizations and declining importance of the West in the world. Let us remember that for this favorite Harvard's son, Latin America is not part of the West. Whether we share Mr Huntington's ideas or not, he provides some interesting data. In particular, those referring to the number of people who watch CNN, which are 52 million or close to 2 percent of the world population. But I think that more important than this fact as such is to try to find the elements which might determine an apodictic future of the world. In this respect, it is interesting Mr Huntington's contention, that the attempt to expand democracy produces the opposite result of a greater antagonism against the West and modernization.

What is then the reality that awaits us in this problematic and dramatic world? It was Karl Popper who said that if the knowledge of ten years hence would be possible today, it would be the knowledge of today. I would say that this dictum of the famous epistemologist should be read as the impossibility of prediction, notwithstanding the attraction that that activity has had throughout history since the times of the Delphic oracles, to Joseph in the court of the Pharaoh. I believe that to try to predict an ineluctable process of progress given the technology and the communications in the capitalist system is just another simplistic approach as it was the planification. On the other hand, I should insist on the fact that the meaning of the West is not only confused but fallacious under the light of history and also at present. To consider the Unites States and Europe in equal terms is a fallacy that *a priori* disqualifies any serious analysis.

If by capitalism we understand the American system, every day it is more obvious the differences between it and what is going on with Zeus lover, even on the Western side, needless to say what is going on in the ex-communist paradise. Some data may illuminate this reality. In a recent paper by Vito Tanzi and published by the IMF, we find the following: Between 1960 and 1994, public expenditure in the European countries rose from 29.6 percent to 45.5 percent of GDP. That is the essence of Social Democracy as had been perceived by Edward Bernstein in 1899, when he postulated that it was possible to achieve socialism through the democratic process and not by revolution.

That increase in government expenditures, as it was to be expected, determined a reduction in the rate of growth, a substantial increase in unemployment as well as a growing public debt which does not meet the targets required by Maastricht for the common currency. At the same time, the inflexibility of the European labor systems and even the Maastricht labor chapter are threatening the viability of the so-called Renanian capitalism, which I would better call «Renanian socialism». Then, we should expect that in the continent will persist the confusion between mercantilism and free trade, which had been clarified by Hume and Adam Smith, but that in practice Colbert and Litz prevail. On the other side of the Atlantic but more of the political spectrum we find the United States. Then, the pejoratively called «wild capitalism» has reduced inflation and unemployment to the bone while increasing the rate of economic growth. Regardless of the validity of my contention respecting the historical differences in the ethic-political ideologies between the Americans and the Europeans, there is no doubt that today there are very different results.

Coming back to our friend, Mr Huntington, from my point of view his pessimism may be right, but not on his terms. It is true that China is growing at 9 percent per year, but it is also true that up to the present what she is doing is copying. Even if they become more or less assertive or belligerent, the truth is that her present economic system is closer to capitalism than to communism. And that is the reason for their success. With respect to the Muslims, the case is very different. Religious fanaticism or enthusiasm is a return to the Middle Ages and let us not forget that feudalism and socialism are based on the same values. What is also true is that that religious fundamentalism may be increasingly dangerous for the civilized world through the expansion of terrorism. That is another case of globalization.

3. Marx and Human Rights

In 1977, Raymond Aron wrote *In Defense of Decadent Europe*. The fact is that one of its chapters was titled «Europe Mystified by Marxism». Notwithstanding that I do not agree with his view over the European historical greatness, I do agree that Europe is mystified by Marxism though wrapped by Berstein under the sacred robe of democracy.

As a proof of that, my initial discrepancy has historical roots. Let us remember the 445 anniversary of Galileo's birthday. In the midst of the Renaissance, Galileo Galilei was condemned by the Church because he had upheld the Copernican theory of the universe. Luckily, he was not finally burned because of the recommendation of Cardenal Bellarmine, who accepted the view that that theory was not a description of the universe but only a better method to understand it. Today the Church has devoted a mass to remember Galileo's birth, though Pope Benedict XVI still appears to hold that the Church was right in condemning him.

Not very far from Rome, in Geneva, another thought creator did not have Galileo's luck. Miguel Servet was burned by a Christian protestant, Mr Calvino, for the sin of finding the circulation of blood. But even more, we should remember that this great European, during The Thirty Years' War between Catholics and Protestants without nuclear weapons and loving their neighbors as themselves were able to kill close to half the European population, mainly in Germany.

But let us not forget either that on the other side of the English Channel, Mr Cromwell in England, forerun Robespierre, and based on better faith credentials before God decided to kill the Stuart King, Charles I. And of course, neither we can set aside the obscurantism of the Enlightenment, when adoring goddess reason, the Jacobins decided to send Luis Capeto, King of France, to the guillotine together with his wife. Following this virtues path, the Jacobins established terror and later on the communes in Paris almost destroyed the city of light.

Then Alberdi, in view of the above events, wrote a letter to Sarmiento saying, «Mr Sarmiento, in view of the latest events that we have experienced, there is an enlightened barbarism more dangerous for civilization than the barbarism of all the savages of South America». And how perceptive he was, that he foresaw what was coming in Europe, as it was very well expressed by François Revel in his book *The Anti-American Obsession*: «They are the European as long as I know, who provoked two cataclysms without precedent that were the two world wars and they also were the inventors and put in practice the two most criminal regimes ever inflicted on humanity».

I have made this historical review because I think that as long as we continue believing in the western civilization as a paradigm of liberty and political virtue, it will be impossible for us to understand the world we live in. And such misunderstanding has been possible through the Marxist mystification that has made the world confuse individual rights with human rights. Such is the hypocrisy and the cynicism prevailing in the world today that Fidel

Castro appears to be a defender of human rights, whereas the United States, to whom we owe freedom in the world, is considered the representative of exploitation through imperialism.

The Marxist dialectic of «from each according to his abilities to each according to his needs» is today included in article 25th of the Universal Declaration of Human Rights. In such a proposal Marx was wrong as much as in his explanation of what he called the «capitalist system». But at least he was consistent in his mistakes, since he assumed that that proposal was only possible to put into practice in the communist society, where liberty prevailed as mankind had overcome scarcity, and so he forecasted the end of history as a result of the end of antagonism.

Then, in *The German Ideology*, Marx described the possibilities of the communist society in the following way, respecting the division of labor: «While in the communist society, where nobody has a particular exclusive sphere of activity, but each one becomes accomplished in any branch he wishes, society regulates the general production and then makes it possible for me to do one thing today and another tomorrow, to hunt in the morning, fish in the afternoon, rear cattle in the evening, criticize after dinner, just as I have a mind without ever becoming hunter, fisher, shepherd or critic».

I have made this long quotation of Marx thinking because I consider really amazing that such stupidity has been accepted and proclaimed by intellectuals and politicians. That philosophy, a favorite child of Enlightenment, has brought Lenin and Stalin and, later on, Fidel Castro to slave the people in their own countries. But undoubtedly if such nonsense of the communist society is a mental aberration, at least as I said before it is consistent with the presupposition that men had overcome scarcity. But today, when everybody knows that poverty exists, it is really a marvel of human minds to have accepted that dialectical approach in article 25th of the Universal Declaration of Human Rights, that said, «Every person has a right to an adequate level of life which assures them, as well as their families, health and well-being and in particular food, clothing, housing and the necessary medical assistance...». I do believe then that we have accepted not the right to the pursuance of happiness, which has been the premise of liberty and consequently of the creation of wealth for the first time in history, but the right to happiness which in Marx terms means the overcoming of scarcity.

A recent article by Stefan Theil, «The European Philosophy of Failure», shows the indoctrination which German and French students are receiving, and so he says, «The French and German schools have collaborated to establish a serious aversion to capitalism...» Capitalism itself has been described as brutal, savage, neoliberal and American. That is why I insist on the fact that the principle of liberty should not be recognized as capitalism. That denomination came from Marx in order to ethically disqualify it by applying the fallacious theory of exploitation. Then, what we are defending is liberty based on the rule of law, which is limited government and the respect for individual rights.

4. Obama, the Founding Fathers and the New Man

USA's financial crisis is not the greatest danger we face, although it has had and is having a recessive impact on the economy. In spite of the fact that the economists with their apocalyptic predictions have turned themselves into the Pythagorean Cassandras of the twentieth century, the American economy was growing at a 3 percent annual rate until the second quarter of 2008. Fortunately, everything seems to show that they are avoiding making the same mistake done in 1929 letting the banking system collapse and shutting down the economy through the Smoot Hawley Act. I can then say that the greatest danger is political and, as Ortega wrote, the greatest danger is the State. And that political danger arises from the possibility that the necessary intervention of the State to overcome the present crisis can be construed as the justification for the substitution of the system that, for the first time in the world's history, has allowed the creation of wealth.

It is in that sense that President Obama's concepts expressed in his inauguration speech can cause some concern. As Lenin said, ideas are actions, and the ideas expressed by the President could be taken into action by this Administration, contradicting the system that constituted the greatness of the US and that he himself recognized in multiple opportunities as such. In a part of his speech he referred specifically to the Founding Fathers and to «our founding documents». In these we find the Declaration of

Independence, in which a fundamental principle is recognized, «the right of man to the pursuance of his own happiness». This founding principle is at the same time fundamental of the ethical conception on which the American political system of the Rule of Law is sustained. It means the ethical recognition of private interests and not the search of the new man who does not sin seven times. Respect and defense of the individual rights (which are not the human rights) are derived from this recognition, and consequently the limitation of political power in accordance to the National Constitution.

Unfortunately, in another paragraph of his speech, the President said, «...the divine promise that we are all equal, we are all free and we all deserve the opportunity to achieve complete happiness». This predicament apparently means the President considers that the currently denominated American creed does not provide that opportunity. It appears to me that we find ourselves here with a contradiction between the right to pursue happiness and the possibility of achieving it. In the first case, happiness is the individual's responsibility, but according to what the President said, the possibility arises that it is the Government who should provide that happiness to those who have not achieved it. From that supposedly moral possibility arises the justification for the Government's unlimited power. Allow me to bring up one of Hamilton's observations in *The Federalist* when he wrote, «A dangerous ambition more often lurks behind the specious mask of the zeal for the rights of the people». I must tell the President that following that line of thought he is confusing individual rights with the so-called human rights. It is, I believe, because of that confusion that he says, «...the question we make ourselves today is not whether the government is too big or small, but if it does work». Supposedly, its operation is to satisfy social needs because he specifically refers to «...help families find work...» (sic). I can understand that due to the crisis, a greater government intervention is required, but the possible generalization of this principle would mean the violation of the principle which limits political power as established by the Constitution. But let us remember Madison's words, «If angels were to govern men, neither external nor internal control on government would be necessary».

By the same token we must acknowledge that the magnitude of public spending is a problem *per se*, that is suffered today by the European Union, reaching 52 percent of the GDP in France and Germany. As George Gilder said in *Wealth and Poverty*, «It is not principally the federal deficit what causes inflation. If the deficit were closed by higher tax rates –and the money supply were held constant-, the price level would likely rise in the orthodox way of the law of costs». But still more, even Marx himself in his criticism of Hegel's *Theory of the State* recognizes the actual behavior of burocracy in contradiction with Hegel's assumption that it represents the general interest and so he said, «For the individual bureaucrat the state's purpose becomes his private purpose of hunting for higher positions and making a career for himself» (sic).

Another paragraph that deserves a profound analysis is the one in which the President recognizes the virtue of the market to create wealth. Notwithstanding this correct assessment of the market, he includes the following statement, «...a nation cannot be prosperous for long if it favors only the rich people». Allow me to insist on the necessity to change the idea of the market for the prevalence of individual rights. This other approach does not mean that those rights could be detrimental to other people's individual rights. It is then the law -justice- the one in charge of avoiding that possibility. Though it is considered that the present crisis was caused by lack of regulations, the truth of the matter is that the speculation in the real estate market was mainly due to Carter's demagogic provision that each American had the right to own his own house.

The credit expansion provided in order to satisfy that demagogic purpose, together with the lowering of the rate of interest, caused in the market what Minsky defines as pure speculation. That is when goods are bought not for use but to resell them. I ask myself how it was possible that those wise economists that today are making apocalyptic predictions were not capable of perceiving that such speculation would lead to create a bubble that finally was going to explode in the way it did? But more than that, we should be aware that such speculation did not benefit anyone whether rich or poor. Fannie Mae as well as Freddy Mac were government creations in order to comply with The Community Reinvestment Act, enacted by Carter and followed by Clinton.

The above quoted paragraph continues with another controversial proposal that will not lead to economic growth, but to the so-called welfare state. That is the prevailing system in the European Union, which has ended up being a «badfare state», as it has been observed in recent articles by Paul Johnson and Dahrendorf. Needless to say how much it worries me the appealing to the common good that it no other thing that the pretention to change human nature. That is Rousseau's proposal followed by Hegel to create the new man, who had no other right than his belonging to the state. The common good, as well as the reason of the state, are the ethical assumptions to justify absolute power in the name of the people and the nation in order to violate individual rights. Unfortunately, this is the present world view that today oppresses the majority of the Latinamerican countries.

The future American foreign policy as it was proposed by the President is also deeply controversial. Mr Obama proposes that the United States should be committed to save from hunger and poverty those countries which today are suffering. Nothing may be more alien to the possibilities of the United States in the world. The wealth of the United States is not a privilege of nature, neither the result of the exploitation of other countries as it was suggested by Lenin in *Imperialism: the Highest Stage of Capitalism*. That was the result of the enforcement of what has been called the American creed (The Rule of Law. Respect for individual rights and the limitation of political power). That is the principle that the poor countries are committed to reject in the name of the anti-imperialism, denominated today as American hegemony. Mr Obama then continues saying, «We cannot allow any longer the indifference with regard to the sufferings outside our borders».

What are then his plans to deal with Cuba, which oppressive and criminal regime appears today in front of the hypocritical eyes of the world as defender of human rights?

And the President continues his speech saying, «Because the world has changed, we have to change with it». I am convinced that the American policy should be the other way around. The one which has to change is the rest of the world in order to be able to achieve what the United States did by the applying of the American creed. If it is the United States the one that changes, then the Americans will suffer the maladies that afflict the largest part of humanity living under the shadows of socialism. And let us remember that socialism was the denomination given by the Enlightenment to demagoguery. In other words, it will be the end of the American dream.

5. From the Cold War to the Hot Peace

In *Democracy in America*, Alexis de Tocqueville wrote, «There are now two great nations in the world, which, starting from different points, seem to be advancing toward the same goal: the Russians and the Anglo-Americans... America's conquests are made with the plowshare, Russia's with the sword».

> «To attain their aims, the farmer relies on personal interest and gives free scope to the unguided strength and common sense of individuals.»

> «The latter in a sense concentrates the whole power of society in one man.»

«One has freedom as the principal means of action; the other has servitude.»

«Their point of departure is different, and their paths, diverse; nevertheless, each seems called by some secret design of Providence one day to hold in its hands the destinies of half the world.»

This antagonism between the plowshare and the sword had taken place twice in the history of mankind. The first one was during the Peloponnesian war between Athens and Sparta and the second one during the Punic Wars, between Rome and Carthage. In both instances, the sword won and since then the history of the so-called Western civilization was written with the sword.

As Tocqueville observes, a new Athens and Carthage were developing in North America under the banner of trade which had been underrated all along. Wealth arose in accordance with this new approach to liberty and individual rights, and the twentieth century witnessed for the first time in history the victory of the plowshare over the sword or more specifically trade over war. The Great War was the first inkling of supremacy of trade and the Second World War was the final demise of the sword as such. As Tocqueville had predicted, the Russian Empire or the Soviet Union became the last challenge of the sword. The actual implosion of the Soviet Empire and the crumbling of the Berlin Wall were the final proof of the supremacy of liberty over servitude.

Liberty created wealth and developed knowledge under the aegis of individual interest, and finally technological development constituted the universal weapon of historical success. Hence the third millennium started in a new and almost unexpected or unpredictable historical setting. From the end of the so-called Cold War, we have passed to what I may call the «Hot Peace». This is not the end of history as it had been wrongly predicted by Fukuyama, but a different form of historical antagonism.

This new historical stage has been called «the era of globalization». The new definition implies to some extent the acceptance of Fukuyama's prediction of the triumph of liberal democracy. In my view, this new approach is wrong because it is based on a mistaken view of the Western civilization. That is, it is not true that the West shares historical values which the enlightenment ended up in the final triumph of liberal democracy.

It was Emmanuel Kant who in his essay «What is Enlightenment?» said, «Enlightenment is man emergence from his self-incurred immaturity. Immaturity is the inability to use one's own understanding without the guidance of another. The motto of Enlightenment is therefore 'Sapere Aude'. Have courage to use your own understanding». Unfortunately, from that very motto surged what I have called the obscurantism of reason. That is, Cartesian rationalism which postulated that at the end reason was the unfailing way to truth. From then on came the Kantian reason in history aside from reason in men's minds and ended up with the Hegelian dialectical process in which reason *per se* closed the gap between reality and rationality.

On the other side of the British Channel, a different approach to the validity of reason gave rise to a completely different and opposing view over human nature. Reason was another imperfect instrument to the difficult road to knowledge, which is always contingent. As Hume had said, «It is from the non-rational elements of our minds that men are saved from total skepticism». Then, we can see that from the very source of superseding immaturity surged a different approach which motto could be «non sapere aude». That is, to acknowledge that we live in a world of uncertainty and that men's frailty is a fact of nature and not the lack of courage to know.

Recent history as developed throughout the twentieth century showed how these two opposing views of the world developed in the final antagonism between freedom and servitude. What we may call the Franco-German political philosophy arising from «sapere aude» or the obscurantism of reason gave rise to the oppressive ideologies of Nazism, Fascism and Marxism (Communism). On the other hand, liberal democracy prevailed through the Anglo-American political philosophy under the consciousness of men fallibility.

Unfortunately, the demise of Communism in the Soviet Empire in no way determined the disappearance of Marxism. Social democracy is Marxism through Bernstein rather than Lenin. Hence we can see that in Europe now including Great Britain through the Labour Party, social democracy and not liberal democracy is the new name of the game. Eduard Bernstein, who should be included as a «master thinker» as the *nouvelle droite* called the German philosophers, wrote the main tenets of social democracy. In his *The Preconditions of Socialism*, Bernstein wrote, «Socialism was the legitimate heir of liberalism... there is no really liberal thought which does not also belong to the elements of the ideas of socialism». This is the greatest mistake of social democracy, because socialism is not the heir of liberalism but its antithesis as Marx very well explained.

Liberalism in the Anglo-American philosophy is an ethical approach to society based on the awareness of the fallibility of human nature. It is for that very reason that liberalism proposes the limits to political power as a safeguard of individual rights. In that sense, civilization is a learning process of controlling the base passions of humanity through justice and property. It is not the reason in history as a fateful process of liberty based on the improvement of human nature. Socialism, on the other hand, is conceived as the historical process of liberation in order to overcome scarcity. This is the Marxian approach and it was later admitted by Bernstein himself.

Although he argued against the necessity of revolution and the dictatorship of the proletariat, Bernstein insisted on the scientific character of Marx philosophy of history. And to some extent, universal suffrage gave the opportunity to social democracy to succeed without a violent revolution as predicted by Marx and acted upon by Lenin. That is the socialization process that we are witnessing in the European Union as government expenditures already account for 57 percent of GDP and the inflexible labor system hinders any possibility of increasing productivity. That is why, according to *The Economist*, «The biggest reason why in the past decade the American economy has grown more than 60 percent faster than

Western Europe and why its unemployment rates have been nearly twice as low is that Europe's product and labor markets have been too rigid, its welfare too generous, its social costs too high for would-be entrepreneurs, its governments too scare to liberalize faster».

The problem is that given its higher costs, it is impossible for them to liberalize because protectionism is the only alternative to the lack of competitiveness. And that is also the reason why the euro has been devalued close to 30 percent since its creation in January, 1999. Now, these obvious philosophical and political differences have shown up in the recent dispute over the 30 percent increase in tariffs and the agricultural subsidies recently granted in the United States. In the political arena, there are even more differences concerning the fight against terrorism and the possibility that the United States could attack Saddam Hussein. If there was any doubt with respect to the European antagonism towards the United States witness the anti-American welcome given to president Bush in his present visit to Berlin.

On the other hand, the recent agreement which will be signed by president Bush during his visit to Russia over the reduction of nuclear weapons is showing an increasing closeness between the two contenders of the Cold War. The organization of the democratic system in a society, which has never known individual liberty, is certainly a difficult task. But it is possible that the present Russian leaders might be aware of the real causes of the lack of productivity of their Communism, which certainly was not because the people did not have the right to vote. That lesson has already been learnt by the Chinese. If that is so, it is possible that Russia will appreciate more than the Europeans the importance of the relationship with the greatest economic power of the world now that, apparently, as Mr Bush recognized in his speech in Berlin, they are no longer enemies but allies in the fight against terrorism.

And terrorism nowadays is the war between two ages. Civilization is facing the destructive power of technology in the hands of the Middle Age mentality. But let us not be one sided. The religious fanaticism is in great scale associated with the fanaticism of the obscurantism of reason as it was explained above. Again, the Europeans have not made up their minds over these two sources of violence and crime. Those who paraded against Bush were not religious fanatics but the other face of over rating rationality as the greens, the pacifists, the anarchists and the anti-globalizers. Certainly, a product of Western civilization. And again, maybe for that reason, the Europeans have decided that the Latin American guerrillas are not terrorists. So much so as General Pinochet was a dictator and apparently Castro is not.

6. Latin American Democracies at Bay

The crumbling of the Berlin Wall and the implosion of the Soviet «empire» eleven years ago produced the impression that the world had finally found the «way». The triumph of liberal democracy was announced and Francis Fukuyama in a well-known best-seller predicted the

«End of History». I am not going to delve into the wrong interpretations of Hegel's political philosophy incurred by Mr Fukuyama, but what we perceive in the world while we are living through the last year of the second millennium of the Christian era is very different from the illusions arising from such transcendental event.

Russia and the ex-Soviet satellites with very few exceptions are going through continuous upheavals, and I would say that history has shown the wisdom of George Kennan analysis of the area made fifty years ago. Western Europe in its strive for unification has been languishing under the burden of the welfare state, which is more the creation of Bernstein's social democracy than Adam Smith's capitalism. Even the apparently successful so-called remain capitalism, praised by Lester Thurow in his *Head to Head*, has been unable to overcome the harmful effect of the welfare state, neither has been able to rescue Eastern Germany from the remnants of communism.

Meanwhile, Japan economy, the other economic giant, is facing growing problems as the system of converting private firms into government dependencies, through a web of regulations, has shown its weaknesses since apparently not even the Japanese are governed by angels, as Madison wisely found with respect to the Americans. On the other hand, the Asian tigers, which for some long time seemed to flabbergast the world with the apparent wisdom of Asian values vs Western vices collapsed in 1997.

And what happened in Latin America? This continent had always been like Jefferson predicted and so he said, «The dangerous economy is within their own breast.

Ignorance and superstition will chain their minds and bodies under religions and military despotism». What Jefferson could not foresee was that more than that Latin America had also been infected with all the European ideologies, which produced statism, in the name of nationalism and guerrillas and subversion in the name of socialism. In any event, even economic theory had come to justify the increasing role of the state in order to achieve economic development. Not least was the influence of Mr Raúl Prebisch to explain the reason for protectionism; the deterioration of the terms of trade, and also of the philosophers of the theory of dependency, who blamed the external capitalist world for the Latin American maladies.

This apparent scientific wisdom was shared by military governments as well as by democratic ones, which in this daring for equality provoked economic and political chaos and created the condition for a demand for order always provided by the militaries. The crumbling of the Wall and the demise of communism appeared to break this vicious cycle of military order and democratic chaos, and one by one Latin American countries started to accept the wisdom of democratic processes and economic liberalism. After eleven years of trial and error, new developments in Latin America show a growing dissatisfaction with the results. Democracy is still on the mount, but the called neo-liberalism is again challenged by the forces of the past, as recession, unemployment and apparent income skewed unfolded.

Developments in Ecuador, Venezuela and Colombia show again the weakness of democratic institutions. The attempt of Mr Fujimori to try to run for a third term in Peru is another threat to democratic viability, while the last year Brazilian devaluation put Mr Cardoso's government at stake in its quarrels with the governors reluctance to pay the state's debt. Needless to say that in spite of all the *fanfarria* about Mercosur, Brazil is still far from an open economy, and it is a common knowledge that growing differences arise with its other major partner, Argentina.

At the end of 1994, Mexico apparently privileged elected Latin American partner in NAFTA and consequently a preferred continental economy of the international financial markets was showed with capital inflows throughout its liberalization and adjustment program started in 1987, which tragically collapsed in the so-called Tequila crisis in 1994.

Apparently, economic theory could not explain this development in an economy, which had reduced the fiscal deficit to almost nil lower inflation to 6 percent from a peak of 113 percent a year, and had been flooded with capital inflows. Moral hazard in the banking system and turbulent political developments were given as explanations for this unfortunate development, which challenged economic theory and more precisely the monetarist approach.

Given the importance of economic success for the stability of the democratic process in Latin America, it is necessary to understand the deteriorating process of economic liberalization, which has affected most Latin American countries. The so-called neo-liberalism then appears to be the culprit of the poor results of the post Berlin Wall economic policies of opening the economy, privatization, balanced budgets and free capital movements.

In the absence of an economic explanation, many other reasons have been given to explain the imbalances generated by the so-called neo-liberalism. One of the most significant ones is the moral hazard in the banking system and the ineptitude of the management to adjust to free market conditions. Another explanation which has been given is the instability of capital movements, which suddenly flight from one country to another. Even Mr Soros, who has invested billions around the world, seems to have accepted this last explanation and his advice is to set domestic controls to capital movements. Others blame monetary and fiscal policy for recessionary processes, and privatization has been considered as the major determinant of the increase in unemployment levels. All those explanations, explicitly or implicitly, are tantamount to blame the free markets for the economic diseases in Latin America. Even when the economy is expanding, it appears to be a growing resentment for the regressive distribution of income and the Marxian approach revives through the accusation that the system makes the rich richer and the poor poorer, while corruption pervades all government institutions.

7. THE ROAD TO LIBERATE LATIN AMERICA FROM ITS LIBERATORS

In 1910, Luis Alberto de Herrera wrote a book, *La Revolución Francesa y Sudamérica* (*The French Revolution and South America*), and there he said, «The inflexible dogmas of the French Revolution commanded to collide against reality. On its behalf and in order every South American society has fallen and continues falling in the abyss of institutional fraud, which leads to the civil war». *Mutatis mutandi* this observation more than explains the continuing failures of democratic processes in Latin America during the twentieth century, which appear to continue in the third millennium.

Evidently, as Herrera had discovered, our historical failures result from the original error of confusing the American Revolution with the French Revolution, which were actually antithetical. More than that, we also ignored the so-called Glorious Revolution of 1688 in Great Britain led by the sound principles of John Locke as expressed in his *Second Treatise of Civil Government* as well as the *Letter Concerning Tolerance*. Hence democracy in Latin America under the aegis of the *Social Contract* was the realm of majority rule ignoring the major achievement of civilization, which was the recognition of individual rights: «life, liberty, property and the pursuance of happiness».

The alternative to the *Social Contract* which through the *Communist Manifest* led to communism was the *Leviathan* which was represented as expressed by Thomas Hobbes by the state which was the «mortal god as inspired by the immortal God». Latin America then changed through its independence from the divine rights of monarchs to the divine rights of the people. No one realized the important finding of Locke respecting the apparently historically ignored fact that monarchs were also men. So he wrote, «But I shall desire those who make this objection to remember that absolute monarchs are but men». But even more transcendental to understand the Latin American political experience is his wise observation respecting political power as such. And so he said, «Hence it is a mistake to think that the supreme or legislative power of any commonwealth can do what it will, and dispose of the estates of the subjects arbitrarily or take any part of them at pleasure».

That was the confusion which so wisely explained Juan Bautista Alberdi in his *Peregrinación de Luz del Día* (*Pilgrimage of Daylight*) between external freedom (independence) and domestic freedom as individual freedom. So he said, «What is the condition of the Latin liberty? It is the liberty of all refunded and consolidated in one single collective and solidary liberty, which is exclusively exercised by an emperor or a liberator czar. It is the liberty of the country personalized in the government and the entire government personalized in one man». That is why Alberdi suggested, «South America will be free when it becomes free from its liberators». This difference between external freedom or independence from foreign governments and internal freedom as individual rights is of major importance to understand the causes of domestic failures in Latin America. As an example, we should realize that Puerto Rico is not independent but the Puerto Ricans are free whereas Cuba is independent but the Cubans are not free.

Evidently, the father of the Argentine Constitution of

1853 had realized the difference between the Franco-German political philosophy and the Anglo-American one, which, as Balint Vazsonyi sustained, are as different as day and night. Unfortunately, not even at this stage of history we have realized this obvious opposition and we insist on the fallacy of shared values in the history of Western Civilization. Argentina in 1853 chose the Anglo-American political philosophy and in only fifty years developed as the eighth richest country of the world at the beginning of the twentieth century. That was not the case of the rest of the Latin American countries, which continued torn between the *Leviathan* and the *Social Contract*.

My major concern is that not only Latin America ignores the opposition between these philosophies but that the whole world appears to have this philosophical confusion as the so-called globalization becomes the new philosophy of history, which in terms of Fukuyama has led to the end of history. But we should remember that, as we already mentioned it, it was Emmanuel Kant who insisted in his essay «What is Enlightenment?» that it was the emergence of sapere aude (atrevete a saber).

That is what I have called the syncretism of Western philosophy and which has politically developed in the so-called human rights. This divinization of humanity as such ignores man's fallibility as recognized by the gospel. In this process, private interests are anathematized, and the state, as the representative of general interest, becomes, in Hegelian terms, the «Divine idea as it exists on earth...». This concept, according to which the state monopolized morality, means that all idea of limited political power is actually precluded. By the same token, this monopolization of social morality by the state means the actual power of bureaucracy to violate individual rights in order to achieve equality through social rights. Hence, the philosophical syncretism was politically transformed into the intermingling of individual rights and their opposite, the social rights, or social privileges granted by political power.

The striving for equality through the manipulation of social rights has produced the worst political mistake, which in the end means the legitimation of violence in the name of income equalization. As Karl Popper had said, «Utopianism is self-defeating and it leads to violence». In my view, this political utopianism comes out of three different sources. The first one is religious fanaticism; the second one is rationalism, which is what I have called the obscurantism of reason. That is the pretension that reason *per se* equals truth. And the third one is political romanticism, which ignores Hume's dictum respecting the fact that there is not such a thing as the love to human kind. Love is a particular feeling, and political romanticism is the universalization of such feeling, as a categorical imperative. I may add a fourth source, which is the ignorance of people and the natural tendency of envy. That is why I have sustained that the so-called globalization can hardly tend to a unified system of common interest, because what people learn through communications is precisely the huge differences in wealth and not its determinant. Little by little, the original European confusion between democracy and socialism has developed since Montesquieu degenerated into a political mess, which has affected democracy in Latin America.

As had been brilliantly perceived by Herrera, that French philosophical and political muddle as rationalized by the «Master Thinkers» has produced the going on civil war, which worst result was the Cuban Revolution. Another illuminating book by the Venezuelan Carlos Rangel, *From the Good Savage to the Good Revolutionary*, describes the political mythology which García Márquez defines as magic realism. But Rangel knows better that we did not invent the myths but inherited them from Europe and so he says, «The fundamental myths of America are not Americans. They are myths created by the European imagination or they even came from afar from the Judeo-Greek antiquity...».

Cuba, in my opinion, was not an exception in Latin America, but the final outcome of this political mythology confronted with reality, which ended in civil war. The difference is that in Cuba the guerrillas defeated the army, that was the exception. But actually it was not. In my view, there are two main reasons that explain why Cuba fell under communism. Cuba had enjoyed a very special economic relationship with the United States, which saved her from the poverty that other Latin American countries experienced and continue experiencing on account of their own ignorance with respect to the main tenets of a Republic, which are individual rights. The stupidity was the same but, thanks to the Americans, we did not pay for it. So the main reason of our support of Castro's anti-Americanism was the gap between our relative wealth and the lack of knowledge respecting the reasons that provided it. We believed to be above the other Latin Americans and of course we assumed that we could challenge the greatest civilization ever achieved in the history of mankind with no cost. The second determinant of this fatal destiny was the fact that the Sergeant Fulgencio Batista and Saldivar had decapitated the Cuban army in 1933. The sergeants became generals and got power with the support of the revolutionaries. In 1959, the sergeants turned the power back to the revolutionaries thinking that they were going to share it, but actually they lost their heads. The United States had two opportunities to revert this setback to Western civilization, but the New Frontier with Mr John Fitzgerald Kennedy at the helm decided to exchange crocodiles for missiles in what Paul Johnson defined as the «America's suicide attempt».

The lesson was learned in the rest of the Continent, where the army notwithstanding their political weaknesses had been the one and only safeguard against the communist assault. At the same time that once and again the guerrillas lost the war against the Army in Latin America, the left under the umbrella of the European social democracy is winning the peace, and the so-called populism appears to be the alternative to the economic failure of the pejorative misnomer of neoliberalism. That is the democratic attempt to liberalize and stabilize the economy and privatize the state enterprises.

Apparently, nobody tries even to recognize that the only Latin American exception to this democratic failure has been the Chilean case. While Castro remains the very symbol of anti-imperialism, General Pinochet has hardly overcome the Europeans attempts to imprison him while forgetting their own historical sins. His main fault was that he succeeded while all the other military governments failed. His success was so great that he changed the course of history of a country and, for the first time in the world, communism won a presidential election. Now, Chile has become an example for the rest of the Latin American countries. But the left once again has succeeded in confusing the mind of the people, associating the militaries with the right and the right with capitalism and the collusion with imperialism. In Europe, they had succeeded in confusing aristocracy with capitalism when actually it was through capitalism that aristocracy lost power. Trade and labor, which are the determinants of wealth, replaced war as the main object of the state.

We insist, however, on ignoring that the aristocratic character rests on the assumption that distribution and not wealth creation is the foundation of ethics. So we come back to square one, and private interest is a priori considered to be contrary to the so-called common good and that efficient production is pure materialism while distribution through political power is somehow spiritualism. So Hegel is back, and the increase in government expenditures is the economic outcome of that ethical approach.

The irruption of the militaries in the political arena of Latin America and in particular the inflation were considered the political and economic maladies which destroyed the natural well-being that the Latin American deserved. The recovery of democracy and the stabilization process followed during the ninety decade, while Latin America collapsed under political upheavals and deep recession, have shown the fallacy of such assumption.

The political problem was not the militaries as such in the same way that inflation was not the economic problem. The militaries as well as the inflation were the consequence of a deeper political and ethical problem which is the lack of juridical security. That is, the ignorance of the rule of law which is the respect for individual rights. Unfortunately, the European example is more and more the main problem faced by the world and, in particular, the Latin American countries which tend to be a farce of the European tragedy. While the European economies, including France, Italy and Germany, collapse under the burden of an overwhelming welfare state, protectionism is again the main threat to the world economy. Socialism is a very expensive way of producing, and protectionism appears to be the only wise and ethical political solution. If the developed economies are fumbling under social democracy it is not difficult to imagine that such a recipe is the main stumbling block to development.

The failure of the so-called neoliberalism was not the opening of the economy or the privatization process as the left pretends it to be, but the impossibility to control government expenditures on the one hand, and the inflexibility of the labor system on the other. As long as we continue believing that distribution is ethical whereas the creation of wealth and profits is materialism, the producers of poverty will always get the votes to be in power. It is the very appeal to the distribution of wealth the main cause of the unequal distribution of wealth as well as the pauperization which comes about as a consequence not of capitalism but of the corruption implied in socialism. As Marx had brilliantly explained in his criticism to Hegel's *Theory of the State*, the bureaucrats convert their own private interest into general interests. Unfortunately, the so-called globalization is a fallacy while communications have globalized information but not formation. That is, the very system that produces the wealth that is known through the communication system is not only ignored but resented by the majority of the countries of the world and not least by the European Union, where social democracy prevails.

Then, it is very important to understand the real nature of the failure of the so-called neoliberalism, because otherwise, the left will succeed in reverting to populism and violence. This lesson has to be learnt more than anyone else by the IMF, which dogmatic approach to adjustment and monetary and fiscal equilibrium has been unable to solve the recent financial crisis in the world. I may say then that, as George Gilder explained in his *Wealth and Poverty*, government expenditures are not part of the product but a factor of production that is part of the cost of producing. Coming back to basics, macroeconomic theory has forgotten the fundamental source of wealth, which is microeconomic and so Gilder says, «Sooner or later, the American liberals like the British Laborites are going to discover that monetary restriction is a wonderful way to destroy the private sector while leaving government intact and offering pretexts for nationalizing industry. Since government has become a factor of production, the only way to diminish its impact on prices is to economize on it -just as one would economize on the use of land, labor or capital– by reducing its size or increasing its productivity». And then, he continued saying, «It is not principally the federal deficit which causes inflation. If the deficit was closed by higher tax rates –and the money supply was held constant– the price level would likely rise in the orthodox way of the law of cost». I would add that interest rates will also rise, and a fundamental disequilibrium would be created as market interest rates are above the profitability of the business sector or what Keynes called «the marginal efficiency of capital».

In Argentina, we have experienced once and again the deleterious results of the attempts to compensate the increase in government expenditures by higher taxes monetary control and a fixed nominal exchange rate. The last experience of the so-called convertibility has been worse because it lasted longer and while inflation is an equilibrating process of disequilibrium, the real interest rate above the rate of return of the system is a cumulative disequilibrium, which finally explodes, and the economy collapses and ends up in a banking crisis. The problem is that utopianism decides the expansion of government expenditures, and monetary orthodoxy is the dogmatic rationalism which is tantamount to what I have called «the obscurantism of reason». This lethal symbiosis of «solidarity» and «dogmatic rationalism» has been at the center of the entire recent financial crisis. We have then to acknowledge that once you cannot control government expenditures neither you can control the nominal exchange rate and the money supply.

8. The Business of Benevolence and Latin American Fantasies

The recent American program to help the Colombian government to fight the drug trafficking has brought to the fore the more complex nature of the Latin American political and economic maladies. For a long time during the second part of the century, there were two simplistic approaches to explain the problem. On the one hand, the militaries appeared to be the one and only reason for the political problems. On the other, inflation was considered the cause of instability and poverty in the continent.

After more than ten years of political democracy and the relative success in controlling inflation in the majority of the Latin American countries, the problems persist under «democracy» –whatever that means- and monetary stability. I am not going to be as apocalyptic as Thomas Jefferson when he said, «The dangerous enemy is within their own breasts. Ignorance and superstition will chain their minds and bodies under religious and military despotism». However, some of his arguments should be taken into account as much as his perception of the difference between Europe and the United States. This basic observation is of major importance to be able to understand the world we live in as well as the causes of the Latin American poverty and political instability.

To ignore the major difference between the Anglo-American and the Franco-German political philosophies is the determining cause of the confusion that we are witness to, through the new marvels of technological developments and the new historicism called «globalization».

Under this syncretism of the Western civilization, it appears that Locke and Rousseau, Hume and Kant, Madison and Hegel, Adam Smith and Marx, among others, are not opposites but complementary. So we accept that European mischiefs are accidentals (the barbarians, the crusades, the inquisition, the terror and the guillotine, the nazis, the holocaust, the communists and the gulags, etcetera) whereas their virtuous pretension of freedom and rights are Occidental. This philosophical syncretism is manifested itself in the political arena as a confusion between individual rights –life, freedom, property and the pursuance of happiness- and social rights, which actually are privileges granted to government which, in turn, are used to violate individual rights. The new name for that political syncretism is «human rights». Equality of wealth, as had been already proclaimed by Montesquieu as the main tenet of the republic, is the traditional European confusion between democracy and socialism. And we are witnesses of the political success of social democracy in Europe coupled with its increasing economic plagues, like the high rate of unemployment and the overwhelming trend towards protectionism.

If democracy is legitimized by votes, socialism legitimacy is based on «equality». Then, as long as we accept this last source of legitimacy, democratic governments are under siege. The guerrillas legitimacy, whether we like it or not, is the acceptance that in democracy the people only vote to decide who are those who are going to continue exploiting them, as Marx had contended. There we have the legitimacy of the Tirofijo, and we pretend to ignore that his legitimation is the ilegitimation of democracy.

But the truth is that even democratic governments in Latin America and in other parts in the world try to accomplish the impossible. That is, to expand social rights (public benevolence) because that has been the road to political power and violates individual rights. And this violation is not only the cause of poverty in our countries but also of the increasing income differentials. Increased government distribution affects productivity regardless of John Stewart Mill and his pupil Edward Bernstein teachings and increases the gap between rich and poor through corruption.

We perceive then that inflation is not the problem, but only one of the manifestations of the real problem, which is the expansion of the government sector at the expense of individual rights. When we finally are able to control money supply and stabilize the exchange rate in spite of the increase in government expenditures, then as interest rates rise, capital flows in to finance the disequilibrium. In the first case, that is, when the government expands expenditure, but finances it with money creation, the system is very inefficient but actually government expenditures do not increase in real terms. And if the government tries to supersede the rate of inflation, what finally happens is hyperinflation, and the monetary system collapses. In the second case, government expenditures increase in real terms and the inefficiency in production is translated into losses of the private sector, as tax costs increase and relative prices change against the producers of tradable goods. Hence the economic system finally collapses as the interest rate is higher than the rate of return of the economy and even more with respect to the producers of tradable goods. The Mexican case during the Tequila is the best example of this process, but that also happened in the Nordic countries and in the South Asian crisis.

Then we are trapped in an «impossible mission». Democracy is judged by results in terms of a paradigmatic heaven on earth. The failure to achieve this impossible dream, which is utopia as Popper said, legitimizes violence. The more violence, more capital out flow, less investment and more poverty, and more corruption. So the business of benevolence is the way to achieve political power, but actually it produces the impoverishment of the masses, which had been forecasted by Marx as a result of the contradictions of capitalism. This wisdom had been found long time ago by Machiavelli, who in *The Prince* said, «For these reasons a prince must care little for the reputation of being a miser, if he wishes to be able to defend himself, to avoid becoming poor and contemptible, and not to be forced to become rapacious...». The only possibility to compete in this world and to take advantage of the globalization is to learn to respect individual rights, something that the Americans learnt in the eighteenth century. That is the prevalence of the Bill of Rights or the rule of law over majority rule. As long as we continue the insecurity of property, underdevelopment will be the characteristic that defines our countries, which in searching benevolence they find poverty.

9. Drugs, Revolution and the Colombian Plan

The president of Uruguay has brought to the fore what we may consider today the most pressing problem in our continent, including the United States: the drug problem and its political as well as economic implications. In general, we talk about Colombia as a special case, but unfortunately it is just a «leading» case. That is, what is going on today in Colombia may be the prolegomenon of what may increasingly happen in the rest of Latin America.

Through «drugs» it has been created a lethal collusion between the mafia and the revolutionaries. Both of them are created by the good intentions of our «moral» governments and institutions. The multibillion business of drug trade is created by the illusion that prohibition is going to control drug addiction. The revolutionaries, on the other hand, are legitimized by the moralist approach to wealth inequalities. The entitlement approach determines the increase in government intervention in order to distribute wealth and so encouraging corruption. The final result is a vicious cycle of more inequality and worse: more poverty. Unfortunately, there are two false assumptions, which, as long as they prevail, the possibility to overcome poverty and achieve political stability in Latin

America are very slim to say the least. The first one is the assumption that democracy as such is the final solution to political and economic maladies. This fallacy is the result of the confusion between majority rule and the rule of law. That is why for a long time military governments appeared to be the problem in Latin America. Decidedly, they were not a solution, but our political and economic problems transcend the arm forces.

As long as democratic governments ignore the rule of law, that is, individual rights, in order to satisfy «social» demands, we will continue the impoverishing path that has characterized our countries. The business in Latin America is not «business», as Rockefeller once said about the United States, but politics and the concomitant bureaucracies based on the pursuance of an impossible dream of changing human nature.

As poverty prevails and inequalities of income increase due to governments' intervention and costs, then a big business shows up: the drug trafficking. The mafia runs a business that is even bigger than the fiscal budget of the majority of the Latin American governments. It is then possible for them to buy the conscience of politicians and government officials, to be able to pursue their illegal trade. Witness the recent case of Peru's Fujimori-Montesinos and Mexico's Lamadrid and brother.

Now in Colombia we find a different approach, which is the alliance with the Marxist guerrillas. The belief that with the crumbling of the Berlin Wall, ideological issues were no longer at stake is denied there. We continue ignoring that Rousseau never foresaw Robespierre neither Marx, Lenin or Stalin. They were a natural outcome of their fallacious approaches to society and human nature. If people are entitled to goods and services just for being alive, then if they lack them, violence is legitimized over votes.

The Americans, however, have decided to consider the drug problem as different from domestic revolutions. Apparently, the drug fight is a moral quest, whereas revolutions are political issues. After dramatically failing in their Cuban, cubanized policy against Castro coupled to the Vietnam syndrome, the United States has accepted what may be called now the Powell doctrine: military intervention is only justified to defend American interest. I do not contend the rational of such doctrine, but the pending issue is how to define American interests. Evidently, the so-called Colombian plan is based on those assumptions. The fight against the drug trafficking is not only moral but falls within the concept of American interest.

The Colombian plan, then, is designed to fight the drug dealers but not the revolutionaries. The legitimacy of these murderers is recognized in the plan given that a share of the money is granted to assuage the endemic poverty which appears to be the reason for the existence of the guerrillas. Another Alliance for Progress? The first one was not very successful as far as I remember, because the revolutionaries are power seekers, and the wealth inequality is just an excuse. The example of Cuba and the poverty of a country which in 1960 was among the richest in Latin America should illustrate the case. And not only that; violence creates insecurity and causes even more poverty. The money, then, gets out from Latin America to Miami, which apparently is the only Latin America city with political stability and juridical security.

There is another part of the problem which this approach tends to ignore. That is, the Americans are not the solution but a large part of the problem. Without the American market, the drug trade would collapse, but that will leave the people in the DEA unemployed. It is then in the middle of this messy situation that the voice of Mr Jorge Batlle, president of Uruguay, claiming for the legalization of «drugs», is not the voice of a drug addict. It is the voice of one who has dared to challenge the «moralism» that makes the «drug trade» the most profitable business all the world round. It is time to listen, because without the support of the mafia the revolutionaries will also disappear. So it will be possible to kill two birds with one stone based on the moral premises of the Bill of Rights according to which to enjoy liberty everyone should be responsible for their actions and not society or the DEA, in this case.

10. Theocracy and Ratiocracy

Some day we will realize the authoritarian and despotic coincidence between the theocracy and what I call «ratiocracy». I have said once and again that in Europe through the Enlightenment the obscurantism of the faith was followed by the obscurantism of reason. During the French Revolution, the Inquisition was replaced by the so-called Committees of Public Health. In time, the reason in history, through dialectical idealism (Hegel) and dialectical materialism (Marx) brought the Gestapo and the KGB. The coincidence between these two moralist ideologies which appear to be antithetical is no more than the pursuance of absolute political power, whether in the name of God or the Divine Reason. Lately this last one through the moralist approach has found in the people the reason for what Jefferson called «elective despotism».

The attempt of President Obama to find an agreement with these two terrorist camps which are represented by Iran in the Middle East and Cuba and Venezuela in America brings dangerous remembrances. In Munich, in 1939, Daladier and Chamberlain put Czechoslovakia in the hands of the nazis, forgetting the Ribbentrop–Molotov agreement between Hitler and Stalin to distribute the world. Later in Yalta, Mr Franklin Delano Roosevelt finely gave Eastern Europe to the gangs of the man of steel Joseph Stalin, better known in the United States as Uncle Joe.

The proposals such as the reincorporating of Cuba to the OAS and the dialogue with the Castro brothers by the same token pretend to ignore the crimes committed by the so-called Green Revolution during fifty years. In this last attempt, it is once again ignored that the unique interest of Fidel Castro is to keep the absolute power that he has enjoyed for more than fifty years. Notwithstanding, the new chief of the South Command of the United States has expressed his worries concerning the relations of Iran in the region. These relationships should not be surprising, given the fact that at present the totalitarian systems only have domestic purposes. I do not believe that in the fanatic heads of Ahmadinejad and Ayatollah Khamenei on one side and Chavez, Correa, Morales, Ortega and Castro on the other, have or had ever had the purpose of leashing a war against the United States.

The fanaticism thread today only concerns to the domestic freedom in the respective countries. The classic example is Cuba, which after the missile crisis, when Mr Kennedy handled it to the Soviet orbit, started to promote the subversion in Latin America, but it never thought to attack the United States. At the time, the Soviet Union was aware that any Cuban attack to the United States would have provoked a nuclear war. Evidently, the politic Bureau did not have the slightest intention to provoke the world holocaust.

It is evident then that the twenty-first century war is the terrorism, and this is not limited to Al Qaeda and Hamas, but the FARC also exists. So exist ETA, IRA and Sendero Luminoso and neither one of them are Muslims. At the same time, the world pretends to ignore the collaboration of Chavez and Correa with Colombian guerrillas. More recently, the cynicism shown by the so-called free world, as well as the Latin American elected despots, has derived and constitutionally disqualified the recent destitution of the Honduras president by the army forces as being a violation of the principles of the Interamerican Democratic Charter. It is my understanding that the destitution of Mr Nixon by the Supreme Court could have been disqualified on the same basis.

The assumed battle against poverty is no more than the excuse of solidarity to justify absolute power and the violation of individual rights. Today falsehood reigns in Latin America, which, under the sacred robe of the democratic nirvana, had replaced the «tyranny» of military governments. For better or for worse, the military governments, regardless their mistakes and excesses, were the only alternative to the communist subversion in Latin America.

The cold war, as an alternative to the world holocaust, is still pending, and unfortunately what we perceive from Mr Obama's foreign policy is that he pretends to ignore that sad reality. There is no such alternative of a dialogue between freedom and totalitarianism. It would be convenient that Mr Obama could read James Madison in *The Federalist Papers* when he wrote, «In a society under the form of which the stronger faction can readily unite and oppress the weaker, anarchy may as truly be said to reign, as in a state of nature where the weaker individual is not secured against the violence of the stronger». And also Alexander Hamilton wrote, «A dangerous ambition more often lurks behind the specious mask of zeal for rights of the people».

Unfortunately, those are the true trends in Latin America, where the totalitarian European philosophy prevails in the name of the so-called human rights and the anti-imperialism. Lenin is back, and consequently every Latin-American government tries to blame American imperialism for the poverty in their respective countries. In the last OAS meeting, the only President who dared to challenge that conventional morality was Oscar Arias of Costa Rica. He entitled his address «we did something wrong», since two hundred years ago we were all poor. That statement was ignored by the press all over the world, and unfortunately a little late he almost retracted from it.

We should not forget either that we owe the ayatollahs to the wisdom of Mr Carter and his advisor and later State Secretary Mr Brzezinski, when they collaborated to destitute the Sha of Iran Rezha Pahlavi. In this respect, we should remember the words of Mr Brzezinski in his book *Between Two Ages. America's Role in the Technetronic Era*. There he expressed his admiration for Marxism and so he wrote: «That is why Marxism represents a further vital and creative stage in the maturing of man's universal vision. Marxism is simultaneously a victory of the external man, active man, over the inner, passive man, and a victory of reason over believe: It stresses man's capacity to shape his material destiny».

Sorry for the length of the quotation, but unfortunately it appears to me that Mr. Brzezinski, who I believe he is also advisor to Mr. Obama was right, if we consider the present world perception of Marxism. More notably in the Western world. So much so that in a recent quest published by *The Economist* said, «Some weeks after the tenth anniversary of the fall of the Berlin Wall the BBC declared that the election of the people concerning who was the most important thinker, the first was Karl Marx and Albert Einstein the second». It is evident then that today belief and reason agree to ignore the fallibility of man, based on the new man (Rousseau), whose only reason to exist is to be a member of State (Hegel). And the most dangerous thing is that as Von Mises had foreseen, those who defend liberty seem to accept the basic premises of socialism as the reason in history and solidarity as the virtue of the new man.

11. Between Cowboys and Jacobins

Some time ago, I wrote *From the Cold War to the Hot Peace*. Today we not only see the warming up of the peace but that on the platform of terror we find ourselves on the fringe of war. I remember that in the 50's John Foster Dulles, Secretary of State of Eisenhower, said, «On the fringe of war to avoid the war». His declaration was disqualified as irresponsible, but the fact was that the United States sent the 7th Fleet to protect Taiwan from the Mao Tse-Tung's threat of invasion. We do not know yet what the final result of this Western quarrel over Iraq will be but what we already clearly perceive is that the so-called Atlantic Alliance is breaking up.

At the time when we do not know if we are actually in the fringe of war to avoid the war or in fact we are already at war, France and Germany have returned to their tricks. In the globalization era, it is easy to be on the side of peace, while what continues being very difficult is the responsibility of freedom. That freedom that the Western Europeans learnt from the entrance of the Sherman tanks in 1945 and the shower of dollars of the Marshall Plan. For the second time in the twentieth century, Western Europe had been saved from the Europeans by the Americans. During the so-called Cold War, Eastern Europe continued being the victim of his historical incapacity for freedom, which unfortunately they always confused with independence, with the prevalence of the reason of state. As Hayek had clearly stated in *The Role to Serfdom*, «The *raison d'état*, in which collectivist ethics has found its most explicit formulation, knows no other limit than that set by expediency –the suitability of the particular act for the end in view». Eastern Europe, of course, did not have the opportunity to enjoy neither Patton nor Marshall and so it went from anti-Germanic fascism to anti-West communism. Today, with the crumbling of the Berlin Wall, apparently they have learnt more than their Franco-German neighbors with Václav Havel at the helm. The war against Iraq and Al-Qaeda or all the way around has accelerated the collision that I forecasted in evident contradiction with the stupidity of the end of history. They want to blame George Bush for the evident brake-up of the Atlantic Alliance as proven by the recent disagreement in NATO. The Texan cowboy could hardly be compared to the wisdom for destruction and oppression shown by Europe throughout history. Let us remember. From the fall of the Roman Empire, they had Crusades, Inquisition in the name of faith, Jacobins with terror and guillotine, holocaust, fascism, gulags, nazism and communism in the name of reason.

Where would we be if the cowboys would not have defeated the Sioux, apaches, comanches *et al.*? Can we think that the buffalo hunters who danced with wolves would have been able to dethrone the Kaiser, vanquished Hitler, Mussolini and Hirohito and contained the Evil Soviet Empire and Mao's China? No, the victory in that struggle for freedom originated in Philadelphia was and will continue being of the cowboys who believe in individual rights and the rule of law and have fought for them and not for those who have arrived to the third millennium based on the reason of state as sublime by the universal suffrage in social democracy.

Already in the 80's another cowboy, Ronald Reagan, defined the Soviet Empire as the Evil Empire and he destroyed it through the galactic war. As Mr Bush today, Reagan was condemned for believing in the philosophy of the cowboys expressed in *The Federalist Papers* but he was able to rescue the United States from the return of the wizards. That policy, which Paul Johnson in his *Modern Times* calls America's suicide attempt, was originated by Kennedy in the Bay of Pigs and the exchange of alligators for missiles by the new frontier, followed by their responsibility of the affluent society and the disaster of Vietnam by Johnson and the final end-up Carter's in naivety and his treason to the Sha and the hand out of Iran to the Middle Ages of the mullahs. It is not surprising that this deep stupidity could have been awarded with the Nobel prize by countries which survived as such without taking into account that they owe their existence to the cowboys and not to the Indians. The Unites States had changed universal history and the very notion of the war. When the United States wins the war, the real victors are the people of the vanquished countries, who, as David Hume had said with respect to the British during Elizabeth I, «...were so thoroughly subdued that like the Easter slaves they were inclined to admire those acts of violence and tyranny, which were exercised over themselves, and at their own expense». Plato had defined the slave as the man who had preferred life over honor. That is, slavery was justified by war and war in the name of sovereignty and reason of state.

From the Second World War onwards, the people defeated by the United States were liberated from the slavery and they learnt not only liberty but also the affluence that had been denied to them by those who governed them. Unfortunately, Yalta determined the hand out of Eastern Europe to Stalin. However, the implosion of the Evil Empire on account of the American nuclear umbrella and the galactic challenge meant the deliberation of the respective people. In 1945 then the United States started a new era liberating and collaborating with the welfare of the vanquished nations. There are the examples of Germany and Japan. With respect to France, in spite of its collusion with the nazis through the Vichy regime, she was allowed to qualify as a belligerent country on the side of the allies. The truth had been the opposite because facing the Molotov-Ribbentrop Pact, the Third Republic divided between Maurras' fascism and Bloom's socialism decided the surrendering of Paris in less than two weeks.

It is not that I am trying to say that the United States discovered universal generosity, but it had the wisdom of implementing at the international level the domestic fundamental principle on account of which the cowboys won over the Indians. National interests are very much more common and compatible than what is assumed by the sovereignty and the reason of state. It was David Hume who in his essay of the *Jealousy of Trade* wrote, «I will venture to assert that the increase of riches and commerce in any nation, instead of hurting, commonly promotes the riches and commerce of all its neighbors; and that a state can scarcely carry its trade and industry very far, where all the surrounding states are buried in ignorance, sloth and barbarism».

By the same token, it would be a fallacy to try to ignore the importance of oil in this fight against terrorism and oppression. Saddam's power struggle does not mean that Iraq is defending its oil rights, but his capacity to destroy a world area where we find the highest reserves of the major source of energy for the development of the people. We should not forget that even though Saddam lacks the power to beat the West as Hitler had before Pearl Harbor, if he actually has the chemical and nuclear weapons, he has more power of destruction than the Luftwaffe with its Stukas and Messerschmitts 110 put together.

On the Muslims' side, they blame the Palestinian struggle for this collision. Actually this is not more than an excuse for the true determinants of Islamic terrorism. As Michael Scott Doran clearly explained in his *Foreign Affairs* article, «Palestine, Iraq and the American Strategy»: «If Palestine is central for the symbolism for Arab politics, it is actually marginal to its substance». The substance is the anti-western attitude of the Islamic people maybe with Turkish exception which remains in the Middle Age, swimming in petrodollars and resented precisely for the historical imperialism of France and England in that region.

Today NATO is crumbling on account of the Franco-Germanic attempt to revive the Holly Roman Empire. The truth is that Turkey is difficult to swallow as part of the European Union for countries such as Germany, where the Turkish born there continue being Turkish and foreigners for generations. So the Franco-Germanic position seems to be less Western than Turkey after Kemal Atatürk and it should not be surprising that so was considered by the Secretary of Defense, Mr Ronfeld.

In the same way that Palestine is an excuse in the Islamic world, the war against Iraq is another excuse in the western world for the profound differences which started more than 200 years ago between the cowboys and the Jacobinism, which remains in the Franco-German soul. The transgenic, the social dumping, the ecology and for sure the differences in the WTO clearly show the prevalence of Colbert and Litz as well as the ignorance of Hume and Adam Smith, which fed the waters of the British Channel. The agreement of France and Germany with the ex Evil Empire under the excuse of peace is no more than the reflection of the long term difference between freedom and the reason of state, which was somewhat hidden during the Cold War on account of the Soviet threat and the dependence on the American umbrella.

12. The Huntington's Challenge to Civilization

Once again, Samuel Huntington has dwelt into an important topic as it was with his last opera magna, *The Clash of Civilization*. In that book, maybe influenced by Spengler, he confused the concepts of civilization and culture. Consequently, he came to some fallacious conclusions, taking for granted uniqueness of the Western civilization and ignoring the deep difference between the United States and Europe. Once that conclusion is reached, I would say it is impossible to understand the world we live in under the myth of globalization. Now, he wrote an essay, «The Hispanic Challenge», which was a preview of the recent book *Who Are We?* In the essay, he again attacks another «civilization», which in his view is threatening the American dream as it had been created by the white anglo-saxons protestants (WASP).

Most unfortunately, Huntington ignores not only the reality of the virtues of his ancestors, as much as the history of Europe form where came most of the immigrants that he likes or admires. But even worse, I think that he ignores the ethical principles on which it was based the greatest civilization ever achieved in the history of mankind, which undoubtedly is the United States of America. I assume that given the fact that David Hume was not protestant but agnostic, professor Huntington disqualified his analysis of the history of England, even though he was not a Muslim or even worse a Hispanic. So David Hume wrote with respect to the situation of the British during Elizabeth I time referring to the Court of

High Commission: «The Court of the High Commission was another jurisdiction even more terrible; both because the crime of heresy of which it took cognizance was more indefinable than other civil offence, and because its methods of inquisition and of administrating oaths were more contrary to all the most simple ideas of justice and equity». And he continuous saying, «In England it engaged the queen to erect monopolies, and grant patents for exclusive trade: an invention so pernicious, that, had she go on, during a track of years, at her own rate, England, the seat of riches, and arts, and commerce, would have contained at present as little industry as Morocco, or the coast of Barbary».

To the virgin queen, illegitimate daughter of Henry VIII, who was the author of the *vincular* divorce by severing the head from the body of his wives, follow the Stuarts James I and Charles I, who tried to put back the Great Albion under the Roman edges. It was during this period when the pilgrims decided to board the Mayflower heading for America. But in 1648 the head of Charles I (I assume that an expression of the superior ethics of the WASPs) was cut off and the power went to Oliver Cromwell, Lord Protector, apparently representing the protestants in the name of the Parliament. Parliament was immediately closed and an ad was placed there «for rent without furniture». That is, until the Glorious Revolution in 1688 William of Orange got the crown of England and it was signed the Act of Settlement, England had the same liberty that was enjoyed in the European continent under the Hapsburgs, the Bourbons and the Horhenzolern. So

Hume wrote, «At that time the British were so subdued that they even appreciate the oppression that was exerted over them».

I should remind, Mr Huntington, that James Madison in Letter 51 of *The Federalist Papers* accepted the Humean principle that justice was useless if men were generous and nature, prodigal. Recognizing the fact of men fallibility as Christianity had established he wrote: «But what is government itself but the greatest of all reflections on human nature? If men were angels, no government would be necessary. If angels were to govern men, neither external nor internal controls on government would be necessary. In framing a government which is to be administered by men over men, the great difficulty lies in this: you must first enable the government to control the governed; and in the next place, oblige it to control itself». That was the role of the Supreme Court, to control the government and protect individual right, that is, the rule of law.

That observation changed the history of mankind, establishing the rule of law over the reason of state. And Madison did not pretend that the WASP morals were superior but he was conscious of the fallibility of human nature in order to change dramatically the relationship between government and the citizens. In this principle, he has taken into account Locke's finding respecting that monarchs are also men. Even more, Madison states that in a free government the security for civil rights must be the same as for religious rights. In the first case, it consists of the multiplicity of interests, and, in the other, of the multiplicity of sects. Hence Madison not only recognized the ethicity of private rights but he also, and according to Adam Smith, does not accept that the predomination of any religion but on the contrary the way to avoid that risk was the multiplicity and not the superiority of one sect over the other.

What is unfortunate, Mr. Huntington, is not the Hispanic challenge which ignorance of the above principle has been the deep cause of the democratic failures in Latin America and so it was in Europe but the threat that represents that the Anglo-Saxons might be forgetting them. There were not the Hispanics who Mr Huntington considers as an inferior race, but the CATO Institute which has been showing the violation of the Bill of Rights in recent times. On the other hand, Hispanics, which undoubtedly is a derogated denomination, are not a race but in any event, a culture. But in the wrong lexicon of Mr Huntington, he believes that we are all a mix of Aztecs and Spaniards and for that reason we are not white but hybrid race but he also forgets that the British are also hybrids of Anglo, Saxons, Celtics and Normans, and I remember that the Romans were there too.

At the same time, that sublime western civilization, in which Mr. Huntington includes France and Germany but not Latin America, was the inventor of the totalitarian systems which have almost destroyed the world, as nazism and communism. We should even remember that those bright European ideas are still threatening Latin America as it is the case of the FARC *et al*. I certainly agree with you that if Columbus had gone to Plymouth instead of the

Antilles, the United States would not have been as she is and I would add that freedom would have failed from the world which would be nazi or communist. But do not take me wrong, the political mischiefs were not invented by the Latin Americans and never in this continent has been committed such abhorrent crimes like in Europe: Crusades, Inquisition, French Revolution, terror, the guillotine, wars, Gestapo, KGB, etcetera.

Even more, I can tell you that from 1853 onwards, Argentina adopted a free Constitution on the same lines of the American one, and even abolished slavery without going through a Civil War as it was the very sad case of the United States. In only 50 years, the application of that Constitution in defense of civil rights changed one of the poorer countries in the continent into the 8th richest one in the world. And this was possible without having to change the religion neither become Anglo-Saxons. The Argentine declination has not been the product of the race, but the way world's influence of the Franco-German political ideas of nationalism and socialism continue threatening the viability of the European Union.

Your analysis respecting the Cuba is also bias by your confusion between civilization and culture. As David Hume said, civilization is a historical learning process and freedom, a luxury of history. Hence, as Vaclav Havel admitted, there is only one civilization, that is, where individual rights are respected and protected and multiple cultures which may or may not be civilized. And remember, individual rights and not the mystification of the so-called human rights that include social rights which actually mean the violation of individual rights and, in particular, property rights. The social rights which assume a contradiction between private and general interests in the Hegelian sense provide the state monopoly of ethics and consequently the omnipotence of the state.

It is my understanding that the Cubans in Florida have learnt or at least have accepted the «rule of law» prevailing in the civilization that according to its own principles has welcomed them. That is why they have been able to create what did not exist and actually Miami has become the capital of Latin America. The proof of the matter is that they were not able to do the same in Cuba. Notwithstanding Castro was brought to power on account of the political illiteracy of the people, we should not forget that he remained there thanks to the «wisdom» of the «New Frontier».

As much as I know, the Cubans have not asked for privileges but accepted the rules of the game, and to that attitude they have been able to reach their undeniable success. That success has also benefited the United States in its relation with Latin America and also with other European countries. It is difficult to find another immigration, Latin or from any other place more attune with your preferences, which could have reached that success in such a short time. On the other hand, I did not know that the Cubans could have asked or thought that the Spanish language should be officialized, something that I believe would be a great mistake.

Given all the reasons that I expressed above, Mr Huntington, your essay is an unfortunate manifestation of racism which certainly violates the Thirteenth Amendment. Then the actual challenge does not come from the «Hispanics» who had not learnt the principles of the rule of law in their own countries, and that is why they are immigrants. The real challenge to civilization comes from the demagoguery of many people who could think as you do, whether Anglo-Saxons or not. My great admiration for your country precisely at the time that we commemorate the sixtieth anniversary of Normandy is because your civilization is the antithesis of your thinking as much as of the Franco-Germanic one, in spite of the fact that the Americans made the French believe that they had fought in the Second World War on the side of the Allies.

13. Bonjour Tristese

It is really sad, distressing, worrisome and threatening to hear the representative of the American foreign policy speak the language of the demagoguery prevailing in Latin America. That was my impression after hearing Mr Nicholas Burns' lecture on American foreign policy in Latin America at the CARI (Argentine Council of Foreign Relations).

The speaker started his address with a reference to the similar values which were shared by Argentina and the United States of liberty and democracy since their origins as immigrant countries. Most unfortunately was that Mr. Burns ignores the deep difference between the Argentina of the second half of the nineteenth century and the beginning of the twentieth, and the present situation where populism prevails. So he ignored the current violations of the individual rights guaranteed by our Constitution, in the name of the people.

More depressing was to hear that the American government agrees with the present Argentine policy on human rights. Hence Mr Burns agrees with the double moral standard applied to the persecution of the militaries charged of committing state terrorism, while the terrorism released by the *montoneros* and the EARP during the government of Peron before the 1976 coup is ignored.

The Argentine Congress under pressure by the president annulled the laws of Punto final (Final Point) and Obediencia Debida (Due Obedience), which were enacted during the democratic government of Mr Alfosín with the purpose of ending the civil war that Argentina suffered during the seventies. Even more outrageous was that this evident violation of the constitutional rights was approved by the Supreme Court, in an act which showed that it was the actual representation of the Court of the Star Chamber in England during the Tudor times.

It is very well-known that Congress cannot annul laws with retroactive effects and even less the penal laws. But even worse was the fact that the nullifying effect has been only applied to the militaries, but not to the revolutionary terrorists who most unfortunately enjoy the present political power as important government officials, in the ministries of Foreign Affair, Defence Economics, Planning, etcetera.

It was also obvious from the speaker words that he

considered that democratic legitimacy is just majority rule, ignoring that the rule of law is the true essence of the Republican government as it was very well expressed by the American Founding Fathers, and so Jefferon said, «...an elective despotism was not what we fought for». Mr Burns even said that he was in favor of the majority and not of the rights of the minorities. Again it is sad that Mr Burns forgot that James Madison had clearly expressed that freedom depended on the protection of individual rights from the oppression of the majorities.

In his appreciation of the present Argentine government, Mr Burns also ignored that the Executive, like Hitler before and Chaves now, enjoys extraordinary powers, granted by the Congress, and even the Judiciary Power is evidently subdued. It is also evident that in Argentina the freedom of the press is restricted and this fact has been recognized by international organizations. By the same token, the citizen is not protected against the arbitrariness of the government, while it is neither safe on the street as delinquency is being justified as a consequence of social inequality. The so-called *piqueteros* (picketers) reign on the street and interrupt transit with impunity. It seems that Mr Burns did not see anything or he preferred to see nothing.

I do not think that it is the responsibility of the United States to impose democracy in the world, but I do believe that in her own interest she should know who her enemies are regardless of the sort of government that they might have. And they should already know that the Argentine government is not one of her friends, since its obvious ideology is the one sustained by the revolutionary terrorists of the seventies. Today Mr Bush is worldwide criticized for having manipulated the information regarding the disposability of weapons of mass destruction by Saddam Hussein. However, it is apparent that that has not been the major mistake of the Irak invasion, but the attempt to impose a democratic system in a society which still lives in the Middle Ages, where there was no separation between politics and religion. What would have been the difference in the actual situation if those weapons would have been found? The first mistake of the Americans in the Middle East was when Carter, with the advice of Brzezinski, decided and supported the fall of the Sha of Iran.

The idea expressed by Kant in his «Perpetual Peace» that democracies do not go to war among themselves is a fallacy. Democracy is not only universal suffrage as it was shown by the fascist regimes of Hitler and Mussolini. Popularity is not a sign of individual freedom. Unfortunately, socialism is the name of the game today in spite of Mr Fukuyama's predictions, and socialism by definition and influenced by Lenin's *Imperialism, the Highest Stage of Capitalism* is in opposition to everything that the United States represents in the world of freedom. If it had been for the Europeans, the world would have been Nazi or Communist, but, unfortunately, to recognize that today is politically incorrect. Last but not least, please do not let down those who in this world and in Argentina still believe in freedom and the Rule of Law.

V. Economics

1. Liberalism and Financial Crisis

It is more than difficult to express the emotion of being here after forty years. In 1959, when the world was crumbling under my feet because of the Cuban Revolution, I was granted a scholarship to study Comparative Law at the S.M.U. That was a turning point in my life. First, I learnt to understand and to admire the greatest civilization ever known in the history of mankind: the United States of America. I also learnt to love the people of Dallas, who were so kind to all of us. And after that, I moved to Argentina and became an Argentine citizen.

But I did not come here to speak about myself but about economics and banking crisis. Apparently, the world has been surprised once again by the Tequila, Japan, the South Asian countries and last but not least the Brazilian case. I have not included the Nordic countries just because I find that nobody appears to pay attention to what happens there. This sequence of events has produced a deep uproar and many people like to speak about the final crisis of capitalism and in Latin America about the failure of the so-called neo-liberalism whatever it is. Then, now we have the wisdom of the third way or better the way to heaven on earth.

Let me tell you that one of the things that I learnt is that there is not such a thing as economics as an autonomous science independent from ethics and politics. And I think that when the Berlin Wall crumbled and the Soviet Empire collapsed, there was the confusion to believe that that was the triumph of democracy over totalitarianism. Allow me to tell you that that was the triumph of capitalism over socialism, and capitalism and socialism are not two different economic systems, but the result of two dramatically opposing ethical approaches to life and two different anthropological conceptions. By the way, the Soviet collapse was not on account of the fact that the Kremlin economist had not gone to Harvard or Chicago. In fact, I have my qualms about the role of the economists.

For some reason or another, the world does not accept the principles on which the American system is based, but they want the results. That is, they want the product without the cost that they call «savage capitalism» or «market fundamentalism». But still the world including Europe is dependent on this «savage capitalism» to survive. And again let me tell you what may be considered a heresy with regard to the orthodox wisdom about the Western civilization. There is not such a thing as a concept of a Western civilization that could be usefully used to analyze the present situation of the so-called West in which, according to Mr Huntington, we, the Latin Americans (not Hispanics), are not included. There is a difference between the European and the Anglo-Saxon political philosophies and in particular the American. To understand this difference, we just have to read the Founding Fathers. Not even after the Americans intervened in Europe in the aftermatch of the Second World War and the Plan Marshall, they have not been able to free themselves from the grip of Social Democracy. That Bernstein invention of Marx without revolution and supposedly without the dictatorship of the proletariat.

I am sorry that I have taken such a long time in the philosophical considerations, but they are the base of the crisis which we fear and those which have already taken place. The world is sick of Social Democracy protectionism and regulations, and the left propaganda is still so efficient that the world blames capitalism and globalization for all the present maladies. Here we have a problem. The right takes the system for granted and cares about producing wealth: the left takes the production of wealth for granted and concentrates its efforts in destroying the system.

Well then let us go to the subject, the financial crisis. And I dare to say that *mutatis mutandi* they all respond to the same causes. In order to briefly analyze all of them, let me explain you my theory, which, in economics terms, we could call «my model». In fact, I am working in a paper with a staff member of the IMF on this subject, which is going to be published soon.

The basic theory is that when government expenditures reach a certain level, the exchange rate is no longer a monetary problem, but a fiscal one. And for a fiscal one

I do not understand a deficit problem but the level of government expenditures. And this is so because for all purposes government expenditures are not part of the product but the main part of the cost of the product. In that sense, I would like to quote George Gilder on his book *Wealth and Poverty*, «Sooner or later American Liberals like British Laborites are going to discover that monetary restrictions are a wonderful way to destroy the private sector while leaving government intact and offering pretext for nationalizing industries». But more important is the following sentence: «Since government has become a factor of production, the only way to diminish its impact on prices is to economize on it, just as one would economize on the use of land, labor or capital, by reducing its size or increasing its productivity».

Gilder found what I consider the crux of the matter. But let us go now to the problem of inflation and interest rate. In my view, in its concern for inflation, monetarism ignored the problem of relative prices. And the problem as Keynes perceived was relative prices and I do certainly agree with him. That is the relation between the tradable and non-tradable goods prices. When government expenditures rise at a rate higher than the rate of devaluation it produces an excess demand in the economy. As government expenditures are mainly consumption expenditures total savings decrease. Then given that the Central Bank does not expand domestic credit, interest rates rise, and the excess demand is financed through capital inflows.

Depending on the propensity of government expenditures to consume tradable or non-tradable goods, the impact would be on the balance of payments or on the prices of non-tradable and more on assets prices, notably real estate. This is the dynamics of the bubble usually created in assets prices or as now has been recognized asset price inflation.

As government expenditures are financed with taxes that increase the cost of production, the impact of this increasing cost is higher on the producers of tradable goods, since they do not have the possibility to transfer their cost on account of the foreign competition. Then relative prices of tradable goods deteriorate in terms of the non-tradable goods and services, notably wages and salaries.

Capital inflow attracted by the interest rates differentials finances the expansion of the economy, as the current account deteriorates. But still it is possible that the capital inflow is so huge that more than compensates this deficit and international reserves increase, and the banking system expands the credit to the private sector. Unfortunately, domestic interest rates in real terms are higher for the tradable and lower for the non-tradable sector. This level of interest rates in terms of the prices of the tradable sector deteriorates the economic situation of the sector. As long as the credit to the sector expands at a higher rate than the nominal rate of interest, the solvency problem created by the difference between the real interest rate and the rate of return of the sector is postponed. Finally, when credit expansion is halted and the inflow of capital stops, the banking balance sheets start to flow the losses caused by the non performing credits. The bubble created in the real state explodes, the capital starts to fly and the economy collapses. This process explains all the recent financial crisis of the Nordic countries, Mexico, South Asia and Brazil. I hope that we would learn this dynamics of the crisis and not to blame the demoniac neo-liberalism.

2. Conference at the Council of the Americas

In a conference of the Council of the Americas, held on May 6th, under the heading of «US Policy Initiative in the Americas», the most outstanding figures of the American foreign policy, including the vice Chairman of the IMF, Anne Krueger, reviewed the situation in the Americas. We can say that the main subject of the conference was the analysis of the failure of the democratic processes in Latin America in providing a successful economic progress to their respective countries. At the same time, all the speeches referred to the necessity to help those countries to avoid any possibility of abandoning the democratic system as a consequence of the economic dissatisfaction. By the same token, the speeches insisted on the need for free trade, and the fight against terrorism and drug trafficking. In essence, the conference considered the situation giving some advice regarding the viability of the system and the commitment of the United States to increase the economic and political support to those democratic processes.

Let me then say something about my deep concern for the misunderstanding of the causes which have determined once and again the apparent failures of democratic processes in Latin America and let us not forget either the European democratic failures in history. For that purpose, I would like to quote one of the Founding Fathers, James Madison, in reference to democratic diseases. So he said in *The Federalist Papers*, «A common passion or interest will, in almost every case, be felt by a majority of the whole; a communication and concert results from the form of Government itself; and there is nothing to check the inducement to sacrifice the weaker party or an obnoxious individual. Hence it is that such democracies have ever been spectacles of turbulence and contention; have ever been found incompatible with personal security or the rights of property; and have in general been as short in their lives, as they have been violent in their deaths. Theoretical politicians, who have patronized this species of Government, have erroneously supposed that by reducing mankind to a perfect equality in their political rights, they would at the same time be perfectly equalized and assimilated in their possessions, their opinions and their passions».

I apologize for the length of the quotation, but it seems to me that in those words we find a better explanation of our maladies that in all the speeches at the conference put together. It should be evident, then, that when we talk about democracy, we are using the same word but we do not mean the same thing. American democracy is based on the rule of law, that is, the prevalence of individual rights over majority rule.

At some point in the speech, Secretary Powell addressed this subject and said, «Leaders around the world committed their countries to sound policies, good governance at all levels, and rule of law». There is the problem; sound policies and good governance depend on the prevalence of the rule of law. Unfortunately, it is the rule of law what is lacking in our democratic process. Let me quote again Mr Madison when he said, «In a society under the form of which the stronger faction can readily unite and oppress the weaker, anarchy may truly be said to reign, as in state of nature where the weaker individual is not secured against the violence of the stronger».

Hence, we may say that most unfortunately our democracies suffer such a disease. We should because that is not a racial or a religious problem, but the ignorance all along of the great difference between the Anglo-American political philosophy and the French-German one. Let me remind you what Mrs Thatcher very recently recognized in that respect when she said that all the totalitarian regimes, nazism, fascism and communism had been the actual product of the continental Europe philosophy.

This misunderstanding is pervading around the world through the mystification of human rights, where the individual rights are intermingled with the so-called social rights, which actually are social privileges granted by omnipotent governments. That omnipotence later on is reflected in the insecurity of property rights and the prevalence of greater corruption. Corruption is not independent from political power and it will be present as long as we ignore the wisdom of Locke discovering that monarchs were also men and, for that reason, fallible. That is the very reason for limiting their power. This confusion is even more harmful if we observe that not only unlimited power is justified in governments, but also justifies the violence of the guerrillas challenging legitimate governments as in the case of Colombia. That is why Juan Bautista Alberdi, the father of our Constitution, once said that «the private thief is the weakest enemy that property faces».

Now, let me address to the case of Argentina, which now appears as the sick man or woman of Latin America, and quote Secretary Powell's words in that respect, «We want to help Argentina work its way out of its problems. Working through the IMF and other international institutions, we remain committed to support additional financial assistance to help stabilize Argentina's economy and put it on the long road to sustained growth. But economic reform alone will not bring Argentina out of crisis. Argentina must also address the underlying political and institutional flaws that encourage excess public sector borrowing, corruption, politized judicial system and lack of transparency in government activities».

I would say that the above description would fit the majority of the Latin American democracies, and it is also obvious that there is not an economic solution, because economic problems always arise from political and philosophical causes. Mainly when people forget the wisdom of Adam Smith's words stating that «governments cannot make the wealth of nation but they can hinder it». Then, if the political and philosophical underpinnings of the Argentina situation are shared with the majority of the Latin American countries, why is it that in this occasion the

Argentina crisis is so deep, so long and so wide? I would say that the dimension of the crisis then is the result not only of political flaws like those which were pointed out by Secretary Powell, but the result of a great mistake in the diagnosis of the crisis, that led to the wrong therapeutic of increasing taxes trying to close the fiscal deficit which actually destroyed the private sector, mainly the producers of tradable goods. Needless to say that in that approach which tried to solve via taxes the evident incompatibility of the increasing fiscal expenditures and the so-called convertibility law which provided for a fixed exchange rate, a bimonetary system full convertibility and the deprivation of the Central Bank of its function as lender of last resort, the Argentine authorities were always supported by the IMF so-called Monetary Approach to the Balance of Payments.

We cannot but recognize much of the wisdom of Mr Powell's words, which were mainly shared by the other political speakers, but it is also necessary to find a new way for solving the present problems, which, in my view, does not correspond with the simplistic approach of the IMF. That cannot be construed as denying the need of the IMF financial help, neither the recommendations to abolish the bankruptcy law as well as the need to change the agreement with the provinces. But we also need that the Fund recognizes that even if government expenditures decline, the private cost will not be reduced as long as the high level of taxation remains unchanged.

The other aspect that should be taken into account is the different impact on the financial system of devaluation when there is a bimonetary system in which more than 60 percent of credits and deposits were dollar denominated. Unfortunately, the decision to devalue, and later on to float, was taken without due regard to this particular condition. Then, the so-called «pesification» of bank credits, while deposits were not, threatens the stability of the financial system. It is for these reasons that we need a new agreement with the IMF as well as a new agreement with the foreign creditors as soon as possible, but taking into account the particularities of this crisis, but not according to the previous approaches which were unable to avoid the storm that was coming.

Now, regarding other considerations, with respect to free trade and the fight to terrorism, we dare to add that the recent increase in agricultural subsidies is not in accordance with the view to have a free trade area. That will give weapons to the protectionism views, which prevail in a large part of Latin America population and certainly in Europe too. The new approach of floating rates as a way to compensate relative changes in productivities among the industrial countries arising from the increase in government expenditures is resembling more and more the competitive devaluations of the 30's, which destroyed international trade up to Bretton Woods. That is why, although I do not agree with the concept of tariff retaliations, I do understand the 30 percent increase of the steel tariffs, if we remember the close to 25 percent devaluation of the euro since January 1999.

I would also like to point out my disagreement with the Cuban embargo. Since the times of Madison's embargo to British products, that weapon has been more harmful for those who apply it. In this particular case, that embargo, which is misleadingly called among the left as a blockade, only helps Fidel Castro to hide his disastrous economic policies and blaming the United States for its mischiefs. Mr Reich's arguments are sustainable coming from a country which is the leader of individual freedom. If American firms wish to lose their money in Cuba, that is their privilege, but then Fidel will be deprived of the only argument that he can use to try to avoid his responsibility. The American policies toward Latin America should not be designed to satisfy the certainly understandable anger of the Cuban community, because in doing so you are putting on the spot precisely the people who most recognize the historical contribution of the United States to freedom in the world.

3. Moral Hazard or Political Hazard

The recent Asian crisis has brought to the forefront the issue of moral hazard with respect to the banking system. My contention is that the «Asian flu» has the same origins as the banking crisis experienced in the Nordic countries and in Mexico. Notwithstanding, the crisis in Asia was more surprising given that said countries apparently complied with the two main tenets of the economic wisdom: a balanced budget and a high rate of domestic savings.

Evidently, the first lesson to be learned is that a balanced budget and a high rate of domestic savings are not sole conditions for maintaining a healthy economy. Although South Korea, Indonesia, Thailand and Malaysia were experiencing a high level of domestic savings and balanced budgets, by the end of 1996, they were running high current account deficits. Two questions inevitably arise: what was behind the disequilibrium? And why was it completely ignored by the financial community, which continued pouring money into the region until mid-1997?

A recent article in *The Economist* cites the reckless behavior of domestic and international banks as the primary cause of the debacle. In his article, Mr Krugman, the new guru on the subject, explains that «competition among over guaranteed and under regulated banks led bankers to base decisions not on a project's expected return but on its return in ideal circumstances», a phenomenon which Mr Krugman has penned «Pangloss value».

Nevertheless, Mr Krugman, never having been a banker, fails to differentiate between expected returns and ideal circumstances. Moreover, most economists concur that the Asian Tigers, in addition to Thailand, Indonesia and Malaysia, had achieved ideal economic circumstances, where in reality, the economies were experiencing an increasing domestic and external disequilibrium.

According to Knutt Wicksell, domestic disequilibrium should be measured as the difference between the real rate of interest and the average rate of return of the economy. Wicksell used this approach when defining business cycles as the difference between the market rate of interest and what he called the «natural rate of interest». I have applied this approach to the present circumstances, when all long-term debt is adjusted by the short-term interest rates.

The disequilibrium in the external sector is caused by the interest rate differential between domestic and external rates. It is this difference that attracts the capital which finances the upturn of the cycle and then produces the revaluation of the domestic currency in real terms. As long as domestic aggregate demands push up the prices of non-tradable goods while the prices of the tradable goods are limited by the nominal exchange rate, disequilibrium will grow domestically and externally.

Domestic disequilibrium is then defined as the situation where tradable goods become increasingly uncompetitive in an expanding economy. Hence the rate of return of this sector is reduced to below the interest rate, which may be very high for it, even if it is low or even negative for the producers of non-tradable goods. Finally, the producers of tradable goods may suffer operational losses, which of course affect the quality of bank assets.

The original losses are not produced by the moral hazard on the part of the banker. The sequence of events in this attempt to compensate losses by allocating more credit to the growing and expanding non-tradable sector including the real estate sector, which receives an increasing amount of credit pushing prices too much higher. As the inflow of capital continues and the rate of credit expansion exceeds the rate of interest on domestic credit, the solvency problem that has been caused in the tradable sector is postponed and accumulated. The inflow of capital in those conditions produces the inflation of asset prices which then rise to a level where their rates of return are lower than the interest rate thus creating a bubble.

On the other hand, as long as domestic interest rates are higher than the international rate, the inflow of capital continues financing the growing current account disequilibrium. A large part of this disequilibrium is due to the trade account as imports rise on the impulse of both the domestic economic expansion and the fading competition from the domestic producers of tradable goods. Of course, the financial services also increase on account of the inflow of capital thus widening the current account deficit.

The market appears to be mesmerized by a mirage of its own making. In spite of the huge current account deficit, the international reserves of the Central Bank continue rising and the authorities consider that they are complying with the rules of the orthodox wisdom. They do not create money, the market does it for them and the banking system continues the expansion of credit that is larger as affected by the multiplier. The monetary base is fully backed by the international reserves while it is financed by the «mirage» of the market.

4. The Dynamics of the Disequilibrium

As we have explained above, the major disequilibrium is the change in relative prices in favor of the non-tradable goods and services, and to the detriment of the producer of tradable goods. This ratio is in fact the so-called exchange rate in real terms, since the non-tradable goods and services are an important part of the cost of production of the tradable goods. The two major components of the non-tradable sector are: government expenditure and labor wage and salaries. I think that in that sense the government is not part of the production in the economy but a large part of the cost of production. Hence given a certain level of nominal exchange rate, any increase in the government expenditures determines a change in relative prices working against the producers of tradable goods. This impact on the tradable sector does not depend on the deficit or the actual level in real term. What matters is the relative increase in cost for the producers of tradable goods, given the fact that they are prevented from transferring that cost onto the consumer on account of the fixing of the nominal exchange rate.

The above illustrates the South Korean case, where government expenditures rose at the rate of 16.20 percent per year in dollar terms from 1987 to 1996. A similar process took place in Thailand, where government expenditures expanded at the rate of 14 percent per year; in Malaysia, 10 percent; and Indonesia, 7.8 percent. None of these governments had a budget deficit and the average rate of saving was close to 35 percent of G.D.P.

In the case of South Korea, the other determining factor of the disequilibrium was the growth of wages in dollar terms. According to the I.F.S. index, nominal wages rose from 100 in 1990 to 213.5 in 1996 and the exchange rate rose by 17.8 percent thereby bringing the actual increase in dollar terms to an estimated 10.4 percent per year. It should be noted however that the wage increase in real terms, deflected by the consumer price index, rose only 7.05 percent per year or about the same rate of growth in real G.D.P.

The problem was the difference between the tradable and non-tradable sectors. It is evident that since inflation, as measured by the C.P.I., was 41 percent or 5.8 percent per year, the increase in wages had an impact on the cost of the producers of tradable goods more than those of non-tradable goods. Accordingly the producers price index for that period rose only 19.9 percent, or about the same amount as in the nominal exchange rate.

Unfortunately, the I.F.S. does not publish similar figures of monthly wages for the other three countries, but it is our understanding that a similar process should have taken place. As such, these two major components of the non-tradable sector government expenditures and wages were the determinants of the growing external disequilibrium notwithstanding the capital inflow that financed it until the end of 1996. By that time, the current account deficit of Korea reached to $23.061 million of which $15.306 million was represented by the trade deficit. In Thailand the current account deficit reached to $14.692 million, and the trade deficit reached $9.488 million. The corresponding figures for Indonesia and Malaysia are not available in the I.F.S. but by 1995 the current account deficits were $7.032 million and $7.362 million, respectively.

Another feature that is interesting to note is that in spite of the high rate of domestic savings and the fiscal equilibrium, all these countries experienced high current account deficits, while their external debts reached record highs. Hence we may say that the monetarist orthodox wisdom did not hold and apparently the current account deficits are independent from budgets deficits or the level of domestic savings. The same facts which explain domestic disequilibrium so does the external one. It should be taken under consideration that while the non-tradable goods sector grew as a result of the expansion of the external as well as the domestic credit, the producers of tradable goods should have had losses on account of the increasing domestic costs. This behavior of the tradable goods sector should have affected the quality of the assets of the banking sector even though the solvency problem did not show up, while the credit expansion rate was higher than the nominal rate of interest, particularly for the producers of tradable goods. Given those circumstances, it should not be a surprise or a manifestation of moral hazard on the side of the bankers that they decided to allocate more resources to the non-tradable sector and, in particular, to real estate. Hence the real estate bubble was developed from what at the time given government policies appeared to be a sound policy from the market point of view.

5. The Nordic Countries

We are aware of the South Asian crisis, but we have almost forgotten the similar banking crisis which affected the Nordic countries from 1989 to 1993. A paper prepared by Burkhard Drees and Ceyla Pazarbasioglu and published by the IMF explains it in the following way: «Delayed policy responses, as well as structural characteristics of the financial system and banks inadequate risk management controls were important determinants of the consequences of the transition from tightly regulated to more or less competitive financial system. In the absence of structural prudential supervision, these incentives coupled with expectations of government intervention in the event of the crisis prompted many Nordic banks to increase their lending excessively».

This is a typical explanation of this phenomenon, in which the culprits are always the bankers' mismanagement influenced by the willingness of central banks to act as lenders of last resort. I find then that in the Nordic countries concurred with the same set of government policies, which determined the crisis in the Asian countries.

In Norway, the crisis developed in 1986, and in 1991 bank loan losses reached 6 percent of total loans. In Finland losses reached to 4.7 percent in 1992 an in Sweden they jumped to 7 percent that same year. Now let us observe the evolution of government expenditures in those three countries. In Norway total government expenditures grew 6.3 percent per year from 263.3 billion kroner in 1986 to 409.0 billion in 1992, while the exchange rate went down from 7.39 kroner to the dollar in 1996 to 6.21 in 1992. Hence the growth of government expenditures in dollar terms was 9.0 percent per year.

Government expenditures in Sweden rose from 641 billion kroner in 1986 to 1.025.7 billion in 1992, while the exchange rate increased from 6.52 kroner to the dollar to

7.53. Hence the rate of expansion of government expenditures in dollar terms reached to 4.7 percent per year. The process in Finland was more dramatic as government expenditures (Central Government), between 1985 and 1992 rose at the rate of 19.4 percent per year in dollar terms.

All these countries experienced increasing current accounts deficits as their respective currencies were revalued in real terms. As in the case of the Asian countries, the capital inflow compensated the current account deficits and international reserves continued growing, although there were some decreases at the peak of the crisis. In the Nordic countries, as in South East Asia, the banks turned to real estate financing and the bubble finally exploded. As we can see, government deficits were almost nil until the peak of the economic crisis, thus the domestic and the external disequilibria could not have been caused by a budget deficit that did not exist at the time. However, there is no doubt that the disequilibrium was the cause of the banking crisis and not the other way around.

6. The Mexican Case

Last but not least the Tequila Crisis in Mexico may be explained in the same way: government expenditures expanded while the exchange rate remained fixed in nominal terms. Therefore from 1987 to December 1994 it may be estimated that government expenditures in dollar terms rose at the rate of 13.5 percent per year. Simultaneously, the monthly wage index rose at the rate of 20 percent per year or 13.3 percent in dollar terms in the period from 1988 to 1994. As these two are the major components of the non-tradable sector it should not be surprising that the producers of tradable goods had been affected by the increase in cost which they were not able to transfer to the consumer. Hence again the current deficit skyrocketed reaching $29.000 million in 1994 as did the foreign liabilities of the banking system. Based on this analysis, it is obvious that the banking system was not the cause of the crisis.

I believe that I have already explained what I consider the genealogy of the recent financial crisis. So I insist that it was not the moral hazard of the bankers or their inexperienced credit mismanagement which caused the crisis nor was the availability of a lender of last resort. The problem was mainly created in all cases by the erroneous economic policies of expanding government expenditures and increasing wages financed by capital inflows, while fixing the exchange rate.

Accordingly, if governments created the problem it is their responsibility to solve it by financing the productive sector and not allowing all the businesses to fail while continuing to expand government expenditures. Therefore we should take into account the conclusion of Kindleberger in his book *The World in Depression 1929-1939*, where he said, «The explanation of this book is that the 1929 depression was so wide, so deep, and so long because the international economic system was rendered unstable by British inability and U. S. unwillingness to assume responsibility for stabilising it by discharging five functions:

1. - maintaining a relatively open market for distress goods;
2. - providing counter cyclical, or at least stable long term lending;
3. - policing a relatively stable system of exchange rates;
4. - ensuring the coordination of macroeconomic policies;
5. - acting as lender of last resort by discounting or otherwise providing liquidity in financial crisis.

Fortunately, the IMF is certainly discharging these functions under the leadership of the U. S. So we should not expect another depression like the one of 1929.

7. The Argentine Dilemma

In his unforgettable book, *Manias, Panics and Crashes*, Charles Kindleberger wrote, «Keynesian theory is incomplete, and not merely because it ignores the money supply. Monetarism is incomplete too». This dictum defines the main causes of the recurrent economic failures in Latin America. In the sixties, the Keynesian multiplier was converted into the twentieth century version of the biblical multiplication of bread and fish. Then, it was created the all powerful Economic Ministry in order to multiply growth under the aegis of the modern version of the Philosopher King: the Minister of Economics. The economists took over. They were full with technical skills but also plagued with a subconscious ideology in which the state was the creator of wealth and their duty to distribute it. So economists superseded the politicians and they became the technocrats who knew how. History shows that under that approach, the final result was always inflation and stagnation.

Then a mystical or mythical reaction to Keynesianism in the form of Monetarism came. His father was Mr Friedman and his dictum, «money matters». Certainly it does, but the new mysticism centered on the budget deficit as the apparent source of all evil. The control of the inflation appeared to be, then, the solution for all maladies, and monetary restriction was the magic recipe. The new gospel read: «Control the money supply and everything else will be granted».

This is the approach that has been applied in this era of liberalization, adjustment, deregulation and privatization. Now, when we perceived that notwithstanding the reduction of inflation everything else was not granted, a new perception but not an explanation arose among the «scientific community». That is the so-called «reform fatigue». According to this perception, the programs were right but people anxieties preclude the possibility to achieve the promised land of development. The fact is that under these circumstances, the politicians feel the dissatisfaction and tend to blame the so-called neoliberalism for the situation. Hence the shadow of government intervention to help the people (and gain votes) is the major threat to the liberalization process.

It was obvious that once we fixed exchange rate the control of the money supply was a necessary condition but not a sufficient one. The other condition is to keep the control of government expenditures and not to increase taxes to finance them. The most recent financial crashes, like the Nordic countries, the Tequila and the latest one, the South Asian, unfolded when there was not budget deficit or at least they had been dramatically reduced and inflation was under control. But in all those cases, government expenditures had been expanded in dollar terms. That is, the rate of increase of government expenditures was very much greater than the rate of change of the exchange rate.

Apparently, Mexico and the South Asian countries as well as the Nordic countries have recovered from their crisis. Even Brazil, which is a special case deserving a deeper analysis, is growing again. But that is not the case of Argentina, where the economic recession persists in spite of the control of the money supply and the price stability. What is then the cause of this Argentine long recession in spite of the world recovery and our magic convertibility? Obviously the dramatic increase in government expenditures during the nineties. Again, the myth of the budget deficit convinced the new authorities that it was necessary to increase the level of taxation and, more recently, reduce the salaries of the government officials. Unfortunately, at the same time that the authorities presented tax collection and the target agreed with the Fund had been exceedingly met, the economy shows a dismal performance. Industrial production fell again in June; households consumption declined and it is expected to decline even more according to the findings of a recent poll; the level of unemployment rose again to 15.5 percent; bankruptcies increased and the Central Bank was forced to close more checking accounts in the banking system.

We think that we should apply a new approach if we are going to overcome the depressing situation of Argentina, where again the amount of people who wish to leave the country is rising. We should remember, then, that government expenditures are not part of the production but a very important part of the cost of producing goods and services and even more important for the producers of tradable goods. This fact was noticed some time ago by George Gilder, who in his *Wealth and Poverty* wrote: «Sooner or later the American liberals like the British Laborites are going to discover that monetary restrictions are a wonderful way to destroy the private sector while leaving government intact and offering pretexts for nationalizing industry... If the deficit was closed by higher tax rates, and the money supply held constant the price level would likely rise in the orthodox way of the law of costs. There would be less investment and production and fewer new products».

Evidently we did not learn that lesson and while we controlled the money supply according to the rules of the convertibility law, government expenditures (provinces included) rose from $37 billion in 1991 to $80.9 billion in 1999. That is, at a rate of 10 percent per year, which means an increase of 10 percentage points of the GDP during the period. And that is why the Argentine peso has been revalued in real terms as the prices of non-tradable goods increased at a higher rate than those of the tradable goods in the first years of the convertibility program.

The force that throws off balance is not then the budget deficit but the level of government expenditures with respect to the GDP given a certain level of productivity. Any attempt to reduce the budget deficit by raising the tax rates reduces the net flows of funds after taxes of the business sector (particularly the producers of tradable goods). Then their rate of return falls below the market interest rates. That is the measure of what should be considered a fundamental disequilibrium, which is not a stock but a flow concept. Then the fundamental disequilibrium arises when the rate of return, or the marginal efficiency of capital in Keynesian terms, is below the domestic market interest rate.

This fundamental disequilibrium is created by the expansion of government expenditures financed with taxes, which, on the one hand, reduce private savings increasing domestic interest rates and, on the other, increase the producer's costs, reducing this rate of return below the interest rate. The one and only solution for this disequilibrium is the reduction of the government sector, but this has to be followed by a reduction in taxes, which is the real burden on the private sector. For that reason, Argentina requires an immediate reduction in the tax rates; a reform of the tax system; a reduction of government expenditures forbidding any new nominal increase in the years to come; flexibility of the labor system; a reduction of the required reserves in the banking system and last but not least a new agreement with the IMF subject to those conditions in order to finance the present level of the budget deficit.

8. Argentina on the Threshold

After more than two months since the Mexican collapse the Argentine authorities have finally agreed on a new adjustment program with the IMF. In order to analyze the wisdom of the new adjustment plan it is necessary to know the nature of the crisis which following the Mexican devaluation caused the withdrawal of 12 percent of 45.000 million deposits from the banking system ($5.000 million). From the very beginning, the authorities pretended that the whole problem arose from the wrong perceptions of the depositors with respect to the Argentine fundamentals. The collapse of the Extrader Bank was construed as a small affair which did not affect the soundness of the financial system, and it had been due to the mismanagement of the institution which had heavily invested in government bonds with short term deposits. Regardless of the validity of the authorities' explanation with respect to the Extrader affair the public did not interpret it in the same way, as increasing liquidity problems were already manifested. The call money rose to more than 50 percent per year, the stock market collapsed and the Argentine bonds fell by more than 30 percent.

The fundamentalist monetarism of the authorities coupled to the charter of the Central Bank which had deprived that institution of its main function as lender of last resort left the market in a sort vacuum which worsened the crisis. As Milton Friedman had wisely said when analyzing the American depression of 1929, «It happens that the liquidity crisis in a unit fractional reserve banking system is precisely the kind of event that triggers and often has triggered a chain reaction». That was the case when the banks were forced to sale their holdings of government bonds at huge losses in order to meet the withdrawal of deposits.

The government insisted on their delusion and considered the crisis as a market misperception of the fundamentals which were still going strong. If it was true that most of the fundamentals were and are still doing well, it was also true that there were some weaknesses in the economic process which had been noticed by the public during the second half of 1994. Government expenditures jumped by 14 percent last year and in the third quarter, the fiscal accounts showed a small deficit for the first time since the beginning of the convertibility program in April 1991. At the same time, Mr Cavallo decided to break relations with the IMF and tried to explain such decision as the result of the improvement in the Argentine fiscal management which allowed him to adopt that measure. The market, on the other hand, construed that decision as a consequence of the impossibility to meet the fiscal targets set by the IMF. Given that environment, it should not be a surprise that the Mexican devaluation acted as a detonator of the crisis.

The authorities deception with respect to the actual nature of the crisis made them be more concerned about the exchange rate than with respect to the liquidity of the banking system, which was the base on which the convertibility program was sustained. Taking the latter for granted, the monetary authorities were reluctant to act as lenders of last resort or intervene in the market to restore the liquidity of the system. So the determinants of the Argentine financial crisis have been: a) the increase in government expenditures which resulted in a fiscal deficit during 1994; b) the impact of the collapse of the Mexican economy after the devaluation; and c) the delusion of the authorities with respect to the nature of the crisis. If from the very beginning the authorities had acknowledged that the major problem was the liquidity and acted accordingly, with a contingency loan from some international institution, it would have been possible to avoid the withdrawal of the deposits which took place. Needless to say that the convertibility law provided the insurance with respect to the exchange rate as long as the public would maintain the confidence in the soundness of the domestic banking system.

The adjustment program agreed with the IMF has two parts: the first one is a financial assistance; and the second one encompasses a tax package, in the expectation that a fiscal surplus of $4.400 million will be attained. It is evident that the decision to obtain a financial assistance was lately adopted, but this is the most successful part of the program. The Argentine government will have an almost immediate access to an IMF loan in the amount of $2.400 million. By the same token, the I.B.R.D. and the I.D.B. will provide one billion dollars each, in order to assist the provincial banks which are to be privatized. The business community has committed itself to subscribe to a new «Argentine Bond» in the amount of $1.000 million but the actual subscription is already above that figure. The international banks are also supposed to provide one more billion dollars. The proceeds of the so-called Argentine Bond are to be administrated privately to provide assistance to the banks with liquidity problems as well as a guarantee to the depositors. There is no doubt that this financial assistance was a necessity to overcome the liquidity crisis. Apparently, the market has already taken notice of the expected assistance and the stock market and the Argentine bonds have started to recover, while the withdrawal of the deposits seems to have been halted.

There is no doubt that the fiscal package had also have a strong impact on the psychology of the market as the Argentine seems to act responsibly in order to restore the faith in the convertibility program. In that sense, it should be considered that in the case of Argentina the devaluation will not solve the problem, because due to the convertibility program the largest part of the loans are dollar denominated. Hence the devaluation would increase in the interest rates and it will add to the solvency problem in the midst of the slow down in the economy. That is why the liquidity of the banks should have been the main concern of the authorities, because as long as the dollars had remained within the Argentine banking system the mere conversion of peso deposits into dollar deposits would not have altered the solvency of the banks.

The actual impact on the economy of the fiscal package may be different from its psychological effect. It is not necessary to be a Keynesian to accept that an increase in tax ratios at the time that the economy is going through a slow down mainly caused by the liquidity crisis will strengthen the recessionary forces. Then it is possible that the attempt to obtain a fiscal surplus may end up in a higher deficit. Hence we expect that throughout the year the government will continue monitoring the impact of the tax raise on the economy in order to reduce it if the expected result is not achieved. In any event, there should not be any doubt that the authorities are committed to maintain the program, and Argentine fundamentals will support it regardless of the above mentioned policy errors. But it should not be forgotten that the one and only solution in the long run is the reduction of government expenditures.

9. Banking Crisis and the Argentine Experience

My subject is banking crisis which appears to be an increasing concern for the international financial system. The recent cases of the S&L association in the United Sates, the Mexican bail out and the present crisis in Japan, France, Italy and Sweden are proof of the importance of this subject.

Most recently there was a survey on International Banking in *The Economist*. There appears the orthodox view concerning the banking crisis which seems to be that the cause of them is the so-called «moral hazard», which is that bankers run high risks because they operate with other people's money. In that sense, *The Economist* quotes a reasoning made by Arthur Rolnick of the FRB of Minneapolis, showing that for the bankers it was a sound gamble to go to a roulette. I also remember what Juan Bautista

Alberdi wrote more than 100 years ago in this respect: «The bank lends with ease for two reasons: one because it gains an interest for the amount lent, and second because it lends other people's money... The use of a thing so excellent and profitable as it is the credit could not be free from the abuses to which are subject other goods as great and profitable as the credit like freedom and power». Then I would say that the banking system is just another challenge to our imagination because, apparently, there is not absolute good on earth. Hence we have to learn to take advantage of the benefits provided by the banking system and deal with the problems that it might create. In that sense, the banking system is not different from the automobiles or any other good which, besides the benefits provided, produces secondary effects like pollution, for example. However, in the first place I am going to contend what I have called the common orthodoxy with respect to the «moral hazard». Though I cannot deny the lucidity of Mr Rolnick's approach, I would say that the recent experience showed that the majority of the problems created in the respective banking systems have not been due to the «moral hazard» of the bankers, but to what I may consider the «moral hazard» of governments.

I wish to remember then what the fathers of the economy said more than two hundred years ago. In his masterpiece, *The Wealth of Nations*, Adam Smith wrote that only a prodigal could pay an interest rate of 10 percent. Well, I would say that governments are our unavoidable prodigals. And it was in the same sense that David Hume said, «Nothing is esteemed a more certain sign of the flourishing conditions of any nation than the lowness of interest».

I do think that the recent developments in macroeconomic theory and the Pitagorean approach to mathematics through the magic of the computers have been done at the cost of ignoring the microeconomic behavior, which is based on the imperfect nature of men, their ethics and their psychology. In that sense, I wish to quote Tocqueville, who in *Democracy in America* said, «General ideas do not bear witness to the power of human intelligence but rather to its inadequacy, for there are no beings exactly alike in nature; no identical facts; no laws which can be applied indiscriminately in the same way to several objects at once».

Now after this long introduction I am going to try to explain what I could consider my model which in view of my inherent modesty I am going to call the Ribas-Wicksell approach. Sorry, I do not like the word «model» to explain human behavior. Instead of the traditional monetary approach in which the so-called fundamental disequilibrium is related to fiscal deficit, domestic credit and foreign reserves, ours is based on real interest rates, government expenditures and real exchange rates. From this stand point, I could say that once government expenditure has reached a certain level there is no longer monetary or exchange rate policy. There is only fiscal policy which has an impact on interest rates and on the real exchange rate.

Let us begin by the real exchange rate. What is the real exchange rate? Well, it is the ratio of the prices of international tradable goods to the prices of the non-tradable. It is obvious then that as government expenditure is the most important non-tradable good, hence whenever it rises, there is a revaluation of the domestic currency. This revaluation does not depend on the level of inflation. It may be caused by inflation, but it is also possible without inflation. The impact of government expenditures necessarily does affect the cost of the producing sector, mainly of tradable goods and services, whether there is inflation or not.

Obviously this revaluation of the domestic currency has an impact on the balance of payment, mainly through the trade account. If there is no domestic inflation, the trade deficit will result from a reduction in exports. If, on the other hand, there is inflation, it may result from an increase in imports. The problem is even greater than just the balance of payment deficit which may be financed for a while. The increase in imports may cause a rise in unemployment as long as the domestic producers are unable to compete with foreign goods as a consequence of the increasing cost caused by the rise in government expenditures.

As government expenditures are mainly consumption expenses in salaries and pensions, it means their level is also the major determinant of the level of savings in the economy. Hence, of the real interest rate. Given a fixed exchange rate, the increase in the nominal interest rate is equal to an increase in the dollar interest rates. The interest rate increases then determines an inflow of capital which finances the balance of payment deficit for a while. The inflow of dollars has an impact on the domestic economy which is reflected in an increasing demand for non-tradable goods and also on the stock market. The first impact contributes to revaluate the currency even more, as the demand for non-tradable increases while the demand for domestic tradable goods declines. The impact on the stock market should be analyzed on its own and it is not my purpose to do it here and now.

But there is another major problem with the level of interest rates which may be relatively low for the producers of non-tradable goods, but very high for the producers of the tradable goods which prices are subject to a cap through the fixed exchange rate. This is what I call a fundamental disequilibrium. That is, when the interest rate is higher than the rate of return of the economy.

The important disequilibrium is not in the public sector, which accounts, at least for a while, may be in black, while the private sector is in red. How then is it possible that this disequilibrium could be sustained for a long time? This possibility is financed precisely by the inflow of capital which determines an increase in total credit, in spite of, or because the domestic credit is checked by the monetary authorities. That is, the expansion of liquidity hides, while it lasts, the solvency problem which is mounting as bank arrears increases. Here comes the problem of the banks and how they fare when interest rates are higher than the rate of return of the productive activities in the economy.

Then I would say that while the present value of the domestic money supply discounted by the prevailing interest rate increases, the solvency problem does not show up. On the other hand, as soon as the expansion of the money supply is halted for whatever reason, the solvency problem appears and the growing arrears might mean increasing losses for the banking system. This problem is more acute now than it used to be, given that long term credit is more and more adjusted by changes in short term rates. That means that the increase in short term interest rates not only paralyzes investment as it was assumed by Wicksell and later by Keynes, but it also affects the whole cost structure of the firm. This may explain the apparent contradiction that appears in the stock market when good news appears in the economy. The stock market perceives the possibility of an increase in interest rates and this increase may affect business profits more than the expected benefit of the expansion in demand.

There is no doubt that there might be inefficiencies in the operation of the banking systems of the less developed countries, but the disequilibrium explained above may arise even in the absence of those inefficiencies. In that sense, I think that it is convenient to analyze what happened in the United States, which banking system cannot be considered of low quality. I am not going to talk about particular cases like the Continental Illinois, but I wish to make a general analysis of what happened between 1960 and 1990 with the American financial system. According to the figures of the I.F.S. the prime rate in real terms, between 1960 and 1979, fluctuated around 0.9 and 1.8 per year. This low level of interest prevailed even during the seventies, when a creeping inflation started to affect the American economy. Hence it was possible for the FDIC not to have to face any major problem in the banking system. But it was in 1979 when Mr Walker decided to suddenly stem inflation through monetary controls. Interest rates skyrocketed and, as it had already happened in Argentina a long time ago, the first casualties were the savings and loans associations.

It is my understanding that the impact of government expenditures on the banking system is more important than the so-called moral hazard: then it is to this problem that we should address all our energies to try to understand it and solve it.

Let me then analyze the adjustment process and the banking crisis. In an article by Peter J. Quirk, «The exchange systems as instruments to control inflation» published in *Finanzas y Desarrollo* of March 1996, the author said, «In the study we came to a conclusion that in general and at least up to 1990, the policies of exchange rates anchor did not produce good results in the region, and they reduced the rate of inflation at the expense of constant balance of payment problems».

The explanation for this result is what I have tried to give above. The fact is that unfortunately there has been a confusion which has arisen from the unconditional application of the so-called Polak model. My major contention is that the balance of payment problem is not created by the domestic credit expansion but by the relative increase in government expenditures which determines the revaluation of the currency. That is the case of Argentina, where at least since 1976 there is an inverse correlation between stabilization and balance of trade deficits. The major example is precisely this period of the so-called «convertibility». My conclusion is as follows: If we admit that the increase of government expenditures determines the revaluation of the currency, then whenever the domestic stabilization (zero fiscal deficit) permits such expansion in real terms, then the result is necessarily a balance of payment deficit.

Hence I may say that once government expenditures have reached a certain level which has determined such revaluation of the currency, there is no solution via a fiscal deficit reduction through an increase in taxes. The iron alternative is the necessity to reduce government expenditures or a devaluation which should have an impact on the real level of government expenditure. It is obvious that if the government attempts to adjust its expenditures to the new exchange rate, the problem will continue while a new one will arise, which is the inflation.

It is true that the banking system is very vulnerable to a process of adjustment like the one we have explained before, but at the same time we should admit that without an efficient adjustment of the banking system (reduction in spreads) the monetary stabilization is not possible. That is, if the cost of intermediation is too high, then we have again the solvency problem that we explained above: that is, the interest rate for the borrower is too high in terms of his own return on capital. The banking system has to accept the condition that the long term rate of interest has to be lower than the rate of return of the economy as a whole. The problem is, as Quirk says in the article above mentioned, that, «When the inflation rate is very high it is very difficult to know the value of the interest rates because the real ones cannot be known directly».

In any event I may say that the solution of this problem does not rest on an increase in the capitalization of the banks. If the moral hazard assumed by Rolnik was there, any capitalization below the total would allow the same gamble but only with different ratios. Never a stock can solve a flow problem, and I would say that increasing capitalization will only reduce the level of credit and obviously increase the rate of interest. In that sense, I disagree to some extent with the findings of the «Corrigan Report» on the Argentine banking system, which says that the problem is the low quality of the bank assets and concludes that the high spread is its consequence. I believe that to a large extent the low quality of the assets reflects the high rate of interest. And as I contend that the high rate of interest is largely determined by the level of government expenditures, the first and more important solution for the banking system comes from the government.

Now if the government is responsible for the real exchange rate as well as for the real interest rate, it is nonsense to try to avoid responsibility for the situation of the banking system during a crisis. And that is what the «Convertibility Law» coupled to the law of the Central Bank provided for by reducing the capacity of the Central Bank to lend to the banks in cases of crisis. That was what the monetary authorities actually did at the beginning of the crisis in December of 1994. However, in their article «The Tequila Effect and the Bank Reform in Argentina» published in *Finanzas y desarrollo* by Mauricio Carrizosa, Danny Leipziger and Hemant Shah, the authors, said, «Considering the magnitude of the crisis, we should remember the merit of the authorities who could maintain the financial system functioning». This criterion is really surprising because the authors at no time try to explain what the cause of the crisis was.

In order to appreciate its magnitude, we may project the GNP growth of the argentine economy from 1990 to 1994 to 1995 which was about 7 percent per year. The actual figure of 1995 was a decline of 4.4 percent in GNP. That means that the cost of the crisis was close to 11.4 percent of the GNP about to $35.000 million. This huge cost of the «Tequila» in Argentina contrasts with what happened in the rest of the continent according to the figures provided by the IMF in its last *World Economic Outlook*. During 1995 the growth of the other countries in the Western hemisphere was as follows: Brazil, 4.2 percent; Chile, 8.5 percent; Colombia, 8.3 percent; Peru, 6.9 percent; Paraguay, 3.5 percent; Venezuela, 2.2 percent; Bolivia, 3.8 percent. Only the economy of Uruguay fell 2.5 percent and it is obvious that the main cause of the Uruguayan decline was Argentina. The authors however insist on their appreciation of the wisdom of the authorities and said, «In spite of an acute unexpected and long recession, the fiscal fundamentals and the price stability remain intact». This comment reminds me of the enlighten analysis of Thomas Sowell in his book *The Vision of the Anointed* when he said, «Indeed empirical evidence itself may be viewed as suspect, insofar as it is inconsistent with that vision».

I think that the analysis of the actual Argentine situation requires an explanation of what were the reasons that determined that Argentina was the only country in Latin America, with the exception of Uruguay, which was affected by the Mexican economic collapse.

The Mexican collapse had the same effect in all the Latin American bonds, which prices dropped steeply. But it was only in Argentina that this fall determined such deep, prolonged and acute recession of which we have not escaped yet. Apparently, it was only from Argentina that $8.000 million or 18 percent of total deposits in the banking system were withdrawn from it. This huge loss of money can explain the recession, the increase of 6 percentage points in the unemployment and the final fall of 4.4 percent of the GNP but there is still a question pending: Why that money was withdrawn from the banks and the largest part of it finally became an outflow of capital from the country?

There is only one reason and it is that the depositors lost confidence in the Argentine banking system. And they did it precisely because the authorities were so keen to keep the ratio of foreign reserves to the monetary base that they completely abandoned the banks at the time of the crisis. My contention is that precisely the nature of the Argentine monetary system, where dollars and pesos are on equal terms the components of the money supply, the key to keep the so-called convertibility lies in the confidence in the viability of the banking system.

When in 1994 the fall in the prices of the Argentine bonds caused huge losses in some Argentine banks, the Central Bank allowed them to go bust instead of bailing them out. The explanation of the authorities was that those banks were no good and that they were precluded by law to act as lender of last resort. They could only lend money for liquidity purposes and only for 30 days and the fall in the price of the bonds was considered a solvency problem which had caused the loss of the capital of those banks.

At the beginning, the public changed their deposits from the wholesale banks to the so-called minorist banks. Then the Central Bank tried to force the latter to act as lenders of last resort to those banks that had originally lost their deposits. The authorities failed in this purpose but they blamed the larger banks for the liquidity crunch. Then, when the public lost the confidence in the banking system as a whole, it started the withdrawal of deposits and finally the dollars flew out of the country.

It was obvious that the problem as perceived by the public was not the exchange rate risk. If that had been the case, the public would have converted their peso deposits into dollar deposits, but they could still keep them in the Argentine banking system. Nothing would have happened then because given the nature of the so-called bi-monetarist system, the total liquidity would not have been affected. Finally the authorities realized that it was necessary to do something to save the banking system from a total collapse. A total of $3.600 millions were provided by the authorities, but it was too late to avoid the effect of the monetary crisis on the economic activity. Even though with the help of the IMF, the BID and the World Bank it was possible to save the largest part of the banking system. But the cost of the delay was the above mentioned $35.000 millions.

Hence it is obvious the necessity of the lender of last resort as had been stated by Kindleberger in his famous *Manias, Panics and Crashes*, where he said, «The 1929 depression was so deep, so great and so long because there was not an international lender of last resort». But it is also necessary to establish the conditions on which it should be based the facility to finance the banks. We could remember Bagehot dictum «when in crisis lend and lend» but he also established a liquidity condition and said, «They should lend only to banks which are solvent but illiquid and at a penal rate».

This recommendation sounds obvious, but the problem is to decide what the difference is between liquidity and solvency, mainly during a banking crisis. In his book *Free to Choose*, Milton Friedman said the following with respect to the 1929 depression: «The monetary collapse was both a cause and effect of the economic collapse. It was originated in large measure from Federal Reserve policy and unquestionably made the economic collapse for worse than it would otherwise had been. However, the economic collapse, once it started, made the monetary collapse worse. Bank loans that might have been «good» loans in a milder recession became «bad» loans in the severe economic collapse...».

It is obvious from the above statement that the dividing line between liquidity and solvency problem during an economic crisis is blurred. Hence there is no other way than analyzing the situation according to its own merits at the time that the crisis develops.

Let us go back then to the Argentine situation. It is

true that the increase in the rate of interest of the United States during 1994 had exerted some pressure on the Argentine financial system. Firstly, because it slowed down the inflow of capital, and consequently the credit expansion fell from close to 4 percent per month between 1991 and 1993 to 1.5 percent per month during 1994. Secondly, because the prices of the Argentine bonds started to decline all along the year 1994, and the Argentine banks were deeply involved in the acquisition of those bonds.

When in December of 1994 with the Mexican collapse the Argentine bond prices fell by close to 30 percent, the banks suffered huge losses in their accounts. Now, is this a solvency or a liquidity problem? If nothing had happened on the liability side of the banks accounts, that is, if their deposits had continued growing or at least had remained stable, nothing would have happened on the asset side on account of the fall in the market prices of the Argentine bonds. On the other hand, when the confidence in the stability of the Argentine banking system eroded and the public started to withdraw their deposits, the banks were forced to sell their bonds in order to face the withdrawal of deposits. On this account, the market price of the bonds fell even further and the perception of the public of the bank eroded the confidence even more.

It is evident then that the solvency problem was created by the liquidity problem arising from the withdrawal of the deposits. The case when the banks had purchased the bonds with margins, even though it is a different situation, at the end it comes to be the same. If the banks had had the liquidity to pay the increasing margins, then the solvency problem would not have been suffered. Actually the face value of the Argentine bonds is what should be considered in order to decide whether there was or was not a capital loss. And this loss should be accounted only in the case that the Argentine government defaults on its obligations. The losses of a fall of the prices of bonds is not that, from the point of view of the economy as a whole as gains and losses balance each other.

Now, once the crisis develops, then the economic collapse actually produces a real loss for the economy. That is, the wealth which was to be created to pay for the interest on the money borrowed from the banks withered away. And it is for this reason that, as Friedman said, «good» loans are converted into «bad» loans during the crisis. As it has been explained, there was no «moral hazard» involved in the crisis, at least until it started to develop. Hence, as Friedman said in the above quoted book: «The FRB continues to promote the myth that private economy is unstable, while its behavior continues to document the reality that the government is today the major source of economic instability».

Lastly I wish to make some comments on the Japanese case. I have left the Japanese case to the end because it appears to be a peculiar one with substantial differences with respect to the previous analysis. However, I do think that, in spite of some differences, Japan responds to the major premises explained before.

According to *The Economist* survey, the Japanese government had socialized the decision making process of the Japanese banking system in order to achieve determined social objectives. In doing so the Japanese case represented a real challenge to the basic premises of the capitalist system, even after the crumbling of the Berlin Wall. In this sense, I want to stress that the so-called capitalist system or, if you prefer, the free enterprise system is not an economic system as such. In my view, there is not such a thing as an economic system in the societies. Societies are ruled by an ethical system of values, which gives rise to political institutions which determine economic results. Allow me to say that the economy is just the export measurement of the opportunity costs involved in two main issues at stakes in every society. The first one is between freedom and equality and the second one between risk and security.

From my point of view, the amazing thing is not that the Japanese economy, deeply biased in favor of security and equality, had finally collapsed but the long time it took to do it. I think that the operation of this system deserves a deeper analysis than the one I can make with the few symptoms that I could find, but it seems to me that the characteristics and the values of the Japanese had something to do with the lasting success of its economic policies.

In fact the Japanese case also appears to challenge Hume's dictum with respect to the level of the interest rate. However, I do not agree with that proposition precisely because the interest rate is a relative concept which has to be related to the rate of return of the economic activities, as I have explained above. Facing an economic system in which, by the government decisions, the business firms are having losses, any interest rate above zero comes out to be unpayable. I know that I am entering in deep water and challenging Von Mises' view with respect to the time character of the interest rate instead of the production concept of the rate of interest. But without attempting to solve this argument I do believe that the very existence of an interest rate in a stagnant economy means a continuing transfer of resources from the borrower to the lenders. Obviously this process has to end at some point or another, and finally we could say that the financial system collapses.

It cannot be surprising then that the Japanese authorities, who were responsible for the bankers' decision with respect to the direction of credit, felt themselves responsible for the stability and survival of the financial system, what is to say the survival of the Japanese economy which is burdened with an amount of credit, which is 105 percent of the GNP. Then we arrive to the same conclusion than before. The problem was not the moral hazard of the bankers, although you may also find some, but the economic hazard created by the decisions of the politicians in favor of equality and security.

Included in the case of Japan is the problem that has also affected almost all the industrial countries, which is the real estate bubble. Apparently, in order to compensate for the losses in the business, the banks turned to the real estate. Once and again we can see that at the beginning real estate prices start to rise and that is why the banks direct larger part of the credit to finance it. At some point, however, the key to the relative increase in real estate prices is the increasing amount of the credit devoted to the sector.

It may sound funny that the increase in general prices is called «inflation» while the increase in real estate prices is called «appreciation». Then the expectation of the capital gain becomes the only reason to divest credit to the real estate sector. Once the expectation of the capital gain disappears, so it does the credit and consequently real estate prices start to decline. This is just a description which we all have seen many times. Now, what is the solution for this process of bubbling and explosion? I think that in this case, apparently, market forces are incapable of avoiding this bubbling process. Hence some controls have to be applied by the authorities. But again no «moral hazard» of the bankers is the determinant of the «bubble» and consequently once it happens, there is no way out but to finance the banks and bail them out. Otherwise the collapse of the economy will be a much higher cost for the taxpayer in terms of lost income.

10. The Washington Consensus vs. the Philadelphia Consensus

According to recent polls, the majority of Latin-Americans feel disappointed after twenty years of democracy. The apparent culprit of the failure of democracy to improve the living standard of the people in the continent has been the so-called Washington consensus. And the Washington Consensus in the eyes of the people is no other thing that the hated neoliberalism, which in Marx words made the rich richer and the poor poorer.

So this is the orthodox view of the left who after the attempts to privatize and liberate the economies has again monopolized what is politically correct. As Rush Limbaugh has said, the left has made political cleansing in the world of ideas. So neoliberalism regarded as the expression of American «imperialism» has been the cause of poverty in the world and particularly in Latin America.

Unfortunately, there are some reasons to believe that the so-called Washington Consensus has to some extent been a major determinant of the economic failures in Latin America. My main contention is that the reason for that is that the Washington Consensus ignored the «Philadelphia Consensus» as the philosophy explained in *The Federalist Papers* and the greatest American contribution to political philosophy, which are the «rule of law» and the paramount role of the Supreme Court.

As Terence Hutchison had said, the success of Adam Smith *The Wealth of Nation* produced a result not wished, which was the acceptance that economics was a science independent from ethics and politics. In mid nineteenth century, Alexis de Tocqueville, in his *L'Ancien Régime et la Révolution*, had blamed the economists more than the philosophers for the Revolution and his main contention was that they had ignored private rights in the name of public utility.

If you look at *The Federalist Papers*, there is not a word about economics. The only concern of the writers was their consciousness of human frailty and the necessary limitation of political power to protect individual rights: life, liberty, property and the right of men to the pursuance of happiness, from the oppression of the majorities acting through their representatives. They had accepted Hume's wisdom concerning private property on which he based the stability of society.

The Bill of Rights was precisely the opposite of the European political approach to power based on the reason of state (raison d'etat) as the expression of the general will through the sovereignty. Alexander Hamilton in Letter 78 of *The Federalist Papers* said, «No Legislature act contrary to the Constitution can be valid». And this principle was definitely established by Judge Marshall in 1803 in the famous case Madison vs. Marbury. In that sense, the role of the Supreme Court as the guarantor of individual rights against the arbitrariness of political power is fundamental.

Nothing of that sort is even conceived in the rest of the world. That is why the character of the United States is not unilateralism but uniqueness particularly with respect to Europe. We should acknowledge that the so-called Western civilization is a historical fallacy based on what I have called the syncretism of Western political philosophy, which ignores the difference between the Franco-German and the Anglo-American one. We should remember that it was Europe which produced the almost apocalypses of the twentieth century, and the creator of the two totalitarian philosophies of nazism and communism.

Without the United States, freedom would have disappeared from the globe, but the socialists insist on the Marxian approach that capitalism is the source of all world maladies. Latin America is not the exception, but the voice of the intellectual resentment for our own mistakes. But do not miss the point that, as Carlos Rangel wrote in *From the Good Savage to the Good Revolutionary*, we did not invent the myths but inherited them from Europe. Latin America is the farce of European tragedy.

Unfortunately, the Americans have accepted by definition that wherever people vote, there is a democratic government, and forgot their own nature with respect to Philadelphia Consensus, which is the Bill of Rights. Where there is no law, as Locke had said, there is no freedom, but not every law means freedom, as Hegel had proposed. The institutions in Latin America are not the means to limit political power, but the instrument of the false ethics of the «human rights» to produce what Alberdi called «the despotism of the state».

Human rights have been the actual result of that syncretism of Western philosophy in which individual rights are intermingled with social rights. Social rights are actually social privileges through which governments are «ethically» allowed to violate individual rights and, in particular, «private property». So the lack of juridical security (the rule of law) is the determinant of the failure of the democratic processes in Latin America in spite of the Washington Consensus.

11. Public Debt and IMF

With default's declaration, and afterwards with debt's 75 percent capital remission, Government has swindled Argentine bondholders. It must be remembered that Adam Smith had already pointed out, «When national debt has been accumulated to a certain level, I believe there is a few chance, it can be completely and equitably paid». It seems evident that Argentine public debt has exceeded that level, almost as financial crisis has affected the world, starting with the Northern European countries.

It is important, then, to enquire among the determinant causes for which public debt reaches the level where, in accordance to the «father of economics», its payment is impossible. At the time, Adam Smith wrote that governments in general had the power to force their subjects into granting them loans. Such was the case of Elizabeth I in England, as David Hume describes in his *History of England*. It is clear that due to such pressures, in reality the debt far from being a loan is transformed into a tax. And even worst, a non-equitable tax. In Argentina, we have recently seen this procedure in Alfonsín's presidential period, when it was established the denominated scheme «compulsory saving». The teachings of Elizabeth I had reached Cavallo, and so we had the compulsory purchase of public debt, for banks and social funds.

From a legal standpoint, such compulsory purchase of public debt titles is a direct violation of our National Constitution, according to its sections 14th, 17th, and, in particular, section 16th, which states, «Equality is tax and public charges base». In connection to our government's political capacity to violate property rights, Alberdi had stressed out, «The private thief is the least of risks property recognises».

It is obvious, from an economic viewpoint, that this violation of property rights reflects the impact that the excessive public expenditure has on economy's productivity. So, returning to Adam Smith, he usually stated, «The biggest nations are never impoverished by private prodigality, but sometimes they are due to the prodigality and improper public conduct». Moreover, he added, «Commerce and manufactures, in very few occasions, are able to flourish in a state where there is little confidence in governmental justice».

However, in our previous analysis, the question that has remained unanswered is: which was the key factor that determined that a great share of public titles was offered in the international market? In a totally free market, without governmental interference, it could be said that such bondholders took a risk, and therefore, beyond government's arbitrariness in public expenditure expansion, they are responsible for their decision. This does not mean government can be released from its share of liability, but does imply that there is a great difference between voluntary and compulsory lending.

Let us explain then what we meant when we referred to a «free governmental meddling market». Anyone who follows free economic principles would encounter after the nineties repetitive financial crisis with the apparently clear fact that financial market's efficiency could be seriously questioned. What leads national and international investors to buy public debt titles of countries that in the end cannot honour them, failing in the process? A risk sign itself is the interest rate, and therefore, the demand of titles should not have reached levels that determined an unpayable debt, in Adam Smith terms.

We have arrived to the core of the matter. The purchase of public debt of developing countries is, in reality, influenced by IMF interference, being demand so much bigger whilst international interest rate is lesser. That is to say, no matter how free financial markets are in those countries, they are not integrated with the international market insofar banks are not indifferent to the margin arising from externally or internally lending (Moreno Villalaz).

It is obvious then that IMF, with its trustee function, produces such integration. In that way, and in accordance with IMF founding statutes, the purposes of the International Monetary Fund are:

ARTICLE 1:
(i) To promote international monetary cooperation through a permanent institution which provides the machinery for consultation and collaboration on international monetary problems.

(ii) To facilitate the expansion and balanced growth of international trade, and to contribute thereby to the promotion and maintenance of high levels of employment and real income and to the development of the productive resources of all members as primary objectives of economic policy.

(iii) To promote exchange stability, to maintain orderly exchange arrangements among members, and to avoid competitive exchange depreciation.

(iv) To assist in the establishment of a multilateral system of payments in respect of current transactions between members and in the elimination of foreign exchange restrictions which hamper the growth of world trade.

(v) To give confidence to members by making the general resources of the Fund temporarily available to them under adequate safeguards, thus providing them with opportunities to correct maladjustments in their balance of payments without resorting to measures destructive of national or international prosperity.

(vi) In accordance with the above, to shorten the duration and lessen the degree of disequilibrium in the international balances of payments of members.

The Fund shall be guided in all its policies and decisions by the purposes set forth in this Article.

From these purposes, it can be observed that the primary function of the Fund is to act as an international auditor and a last instance loaner. In particular, SECTION (v) OF ARTICLE I implies IMF represents the «certification» that the payment system of the given country can be trusted, in connection with its assumed commitments and its economy equilibrium. Therefore, once the IMF approves an agreement, it generates the necessary confidence in the market so as to permit the given government to place public debt in it.

The remaining problem to elucidate is whether the government has fulfilled or not mentioned section v, regarding the granting of «safeguards, thus providing them with opportunity to correct maladjustments in their balance of payments». These safeguards are denominated «goals» in loan agreements with IMF, and are fundamentally referred to the determination of the fiscal deficit in connection to the GDP and to the expansion of the net domestic credit. These policies were established by Polack in 1956 through its paper «Monetary Analysis of Income Formation and Payments Problems». The mentioned author says, «Economic development could have been financed with higher taxes or with foreign loans. In such situations, the desire of spending for a particular reason would not have produced problems of payment. In a real sense, credit expansion is the cause of payments problems». This criterion, denominated «Monetary approach of the Balance of Payments», sets the basis for the IMF policies. The Monetary approach of the Balance of Payments, originally posed, is developed from a basic error. It is not true, payments problems do not arise whenever domestic credit is not expanded and the fiscal deficit is financed with higher taxes or foreign credits. In the first place, the increase of taxes produces an increment of production costs, whose impact is larger in the case of exchangeable goods. Therefore, depending on how high is the rise, manufacturers of exchangeable goods are not able to compete with foreign competitors, and consequently imports increase and exports decrease. In the second place, if it is financed with foreign credit, with higher interest rates than those existing in the international market and superior even to the Return Interest Rate of productive activities (particularly of exchangeable goods), a debt that cannot be paid is created, together with a decrease in the level of tax collection. As a consequence, fiscal deficit grows due to the increment of the public spending, as a result of the payments of debt interests.

This problem has been explained by George Gilder in «Wealth and Poverty» when he states, «Sooner or later American liberals, such as British laborists, will discover that monetary restrictions are a marvellous way of destroying private sector, leaving the government intact and offering pretexts for industry nationalisation. Given the fact, government has become a new factor of production, the unique manner of diminishing its impact over prices is economising, as much as it would be economised in factors as land, labor and capital, reducing its size and increasing productivity».

Under IMF's influence, it was allowed that nothing was made in connection to spending and therefore, deficit and monetary control were emphasised. And in connection to this, Gilder says, «To say that the Federal Reserve does not have to accommodate governmental expenditure is to say that private sector must pay... The victim will be the future, the vital investments of the free enterprise and the creative forces of the possible real growth and market's necessary resources for new production. If deficit was eliminated with higher taxes and the monetary supply was constant, the level of prices would increase in the orthodox manner, of costs law».

It was grounded in such criteria that the IMF policies were developed and that financial crises were produced in the nineties, particularly in Argentina. In our case, at the beginning of 2000, IMF approved the increment of tax rates (the «impuestazo»). The result of such policy, in that year, was not authorities' failure with IMF recommendations regarding «tax increase» and «no expansion of domestic expenditure». The goals were not fulfilled because it happened what Adam Smith had early observed: the increment in tax rates did not raise the level of tax collection. We can notice that «impuestazo» produced a small increment that recovered the level of collection reached in 1998. Despite the reduction of primary expenditure, consolidated at $2.618 millions, the total deficit, included interests, reached $10.000 million 3.5 percent of GDP. The impact of such tax rise had its effects in the productive system, and the GDP fell near 1 percent during the year. At the same time, the government fulfilled the goals of domestic credit expansion and maintenance of a low rate of exchange, while minimum cash requirements reached 20 or 21 percent of the deposits. This policy of high reserves at the same time the public expenditure level remained high (29 percent of GDP) as well, increased interests rates to «unpayable levels», and in fact we could say the hole banking system was potentially broke.

It must be taken into consideration that those programs were implemented by Menem and De la Rua's administrations and were *approved* by IMF. In March 2000, IMF approved a standby agreement of $7.200 million, for three years, after the erroneous and absurd «impuestazo» of Machinea, based on the «fiscal effort wisdom». An IMF press release said, «The reinforcement of public finances includes an expenditure restriction, a significant effort in taxation and measures to strengthen the tax administration». At the same time, based upon who knows what reasons, IMF assumed that GDP would increase a 3.5 percent. Of course, from such generalities, it continued saying that the consolidated deficit would be reduced in 3¾ percent of GDP and obviously such monetarist myopia did not foresee that an increment in tax rates would reduce tax collection in general.

In January 2001, during the second review of the standby agreement, IMF considered that the problem of the Argentine economy was recession, and that it had caused a reduction of credits demand. Next, IMF explains the continuity of the recession during 2000 as a reflection of the fiscal adjustment impact on demand, but mainly by a fall in consumers and enterprises confidence and expectations due to the increasingly international financial difficulties. The general analyses of IMF explain the Argentine situation by causes foreign to government policies, and, in some cases, to factors beyond its control. Notwithstanding this situation, at this moment, IMF confides in the soundness of the banking system and convinced with Central Bank's authorities wisdom, appointed, «The banking system continues highly capitalised with adequate relation of capital (Basilea's criteria) of 20.2 percent and maintains high levels of liquidity. The international liquid reserves are equivalent to 20 percent of the total deposits, a coverage that reaches 28 percent, if included the contingent credit with foreign banks».

The IMF recognises that the new government had maintained a firm control of expenditure not included interests, but the deficit still grew as a consequence of the drop in tax collection. Likewise, ignoring the real causes of recession insists that authorities, aware of the necessity of a demand and investment reactivation, would carry out a plan to achieve such goal, including the elimination and reduction of taxes. Then, Staff recommended Stand By agreement should increase up to a 500 percent of the installment (Suplemental Resource Facility), and it was achieved the mentioned «blindaje». In September 2001, IMF again increased the credit given in March 2000, and increased in January 2001, in $21.000 million. At that moment, Miss Anne Krueger, so criticised in Argentina, expressed, «IMF appreciates the strengthening of fiscal effort in the reformulated program of Argentine authorities that must restore the macroeconomic stability and remove structural obstacles to investment and production recuperation. The reinforced program aims to restore fiscal policies credibility and the convertibility regime through a fiscal policy directed to the immediate elimination of federal government's deficit, as it was commanded by deficit zero statute, approved by Congress in July 2001. The Provincial states governments are expected to make a substantial fiscal adjustment. The convertibility regime and the banking system liquid defenses are mainstays of country's economic strategy and have been vital to face financial conditions. Therefore the Fund appreciates the reaffirmation of authorities with its compromise to those policies».

After the sequence of mistakes that commenced with Miss Ter-Minassian and ended with the Miss Krueger's belief on deficit zero superstition, the Fund could hardly be surprised that we ended up in the «corralito». The worst thing this Argentine policy agreed with IMF has produced, based on increasing public expenditure and taxes whilst maintaining the fix exchange rate pegged to dollar par «wisdom», has been having given leftists all necessary elements to consider the present situation as a consequence of neoliberalism. In reality, Argentine crisis, as well as those that stroke Brazil, Mexico, Asia and north European countries, was due to the incompatibility of policies such as increasing public expenditure and taxes, with a fix rate of exchange. The process in Argentina was even worst, given the bimonetary system more dollarized at every moment, based upon an assumption that stability and security of the banking system were guaranteed by the convertibility act. When banking system's solvency was threatened by State bankruptcy and the lack of enterprise profitability, there was no sufficient level of liquidity to avoid the stampede. The «corralito» was *the consequence*; the savers that had believed authorities and IMF were logically disappointed, even though in many cases they missed placing liabilities or blaming banks. The last ones have been harmed as well, by an apparent stability and an increasingly disequilibrium caused by the clear political insecurity.

Taking into consideration all the above said, we can conclude that liability should exclusively be placed upon the National Government in the case of banks and social funds, but not totally in the case of Argentine international bonds holders that purchased in the international market. In the second case, IMF must face joint liability with National Government for the caused damage. It is obvious and the likeliest of all that without the intervention of IMF market would not have facilitated funds to Argentina in the amount that it did. I believe it has been proven that the convertibility regime's failure did not result from government's failure to fulfill IMF policies and goals. There they lay all public statements of IMF and its functionaries, in every opportunity the loan agreements were approved with Argentina. And for more evidence of such liability, Miss Krueger declared in her many public statements, in March 2002 and during 2001, that Argentine currency, the peso, was overvalued and that the country itself was carrying an excessive debt. These words, in contrast with those quoted before, when Argentina was granted with an $8.000 million loan in August of that year.

It is not possible then that an international entity, whose policy must be designed to attain confidence, incurs in the appointed errors and is totally irresponsible from a judicial standpoint, towards the savers that it induced to purchase Argentine bonds. Therefore, given that USA courts have admitted Argentine bonds holders' actions against National Government, it can be sustained that IMF must suffer the same fate. If not, what would be the purpose of the existence of the international entity, if its policies do not help countries in crisis, but do encourage national and international savers to incur in great losses?

12. Sustainable Development and the Precautionary Principle

> «We have seen virtue flee as the light of the arts and sciences rose above our horizon, and the same phenomenon has been observed in all times and places.»
>
> Jean-Jacques Rousseau; *Essay on: Has the restoration of the arts and sciences been conducive to the purification of morals?*

> «Thus industry, knowledge and humanity are linked together by and indissoluble chain and are found, from experience as well as reason, to be peculiar to the more polished and what are commonly denominated the more luxurious ages.»
>
> David Hume; *Of Refinements in the Arts*

From the above quotations, we can see fairly clear that the Enlightenment gave rise to two completely different and contradictory philosophies. Unfortunately, a historical syncretism of the Western philosophy has hindered the possibility to understand the true tenets of the freedom and well-being that we enjoy in the West. That is the nature and conditions which underlay the so-called open society and economic development

That philosophical antagonism has reappeared in the prevailing issues over the environment. On this subject it is perceived again the apparent collision between individual rights and the general interest or common good. In this new Armageddon, it is not possible to overstate the decisive role of domestic and international bureaucracies. It seems that we have forgotten the clever Marx criticism of bureaucracies included in his «Critique of Hegel's Philosophy of the State». There he wrote, «In bureaucracy the identity of the state's interest and particular private purpose is established in such a way that the state's interest becomes a particular private purpose opposed to other private purposes... For the bureaucrat, the world is a mere object of his concern». Obviously the above remarks could be extended to the international bureaucracies.

We can see, then, that philosophical antagonism develops into the antagonism between romanticism and civilization (nature vs. art and science) and the one between private interest and the general interest (the individual vs. society). From them come the principles of «sustainable development» and the «precautionary principle». The first one implies that economic development should be restricted in accordance to the limits of disposable resources at the state of the art; and the second determines that technological change should be accepted provided that no damage could be done to the environment.

According to Simon Kuznets, economic development started about 250 years ago. He then reasoned that «if per capita product had grown 15 percent per decade for three centuries before the 1960s, per capita product in the 1660s would have been 1/66th of the present level. But a per capita income at even a twentieth of the present levels could not have sustained the population of even the most developed countries». Then it is obvious that economic growth started with the acknowledgement of individual rights in Great Britain and a little later in the United States. And that is the Anglo-American philosophy but not the Franco-German one in spite of Luther and Calvin. And this development was the result of the advancement in knowledge.

But what is development then, if not technological change based on the improvement in knowledge? The very concept of natural resources is certainly misleading. Natural resources are not resources as long as they are natural. Let us take for example the case of oil. Without the steam machine and the engine, the Arabs would have continued starving looking for water while floating on a sea of oil. Notwithstanding nature has a good press while artifice (man art) does not. Hence, the contrast between the romanticism prevailing in values while materialism conditions our behavior constitutes the major threat to the freedom and well-being achieved in the so-called open society. This human dichotomy has its major representation in bureaucracies which materialism is based on general romanticism.

Then, the very concept of sustainable development, as conceived by bureaucracies around the world with the new greens -ex reds- is fallacious, since it ignores the very nature of development. That is, the expansion of knowledge and technological change. Hence, all predictions based on the state of the art are doomed to fail. Moreover, when the precautionary principle restricts the very possibility of technological change.

Almost two hundred years ago, Thomas Malthus published his famous *An Essay on the Principle of Population* and predicted that stagnation was the future of humanity. His prediction was based on his historical analysis, which revealed that while unchecked population tended to grow exponentially, food supply increased arithmetically. Obviously his analysis was necessarily based on the state of the scientific and technological knowledge of his time. What he could not predict was precisely the determining factor of development, that is, the advance of knowledge, which finally refuted his theory.

Again, at the end of the last century, a new prediction became popular. Cities were going to crumble under the weight of the excrement of the horses needed for transport. Of course the automobile industry had not started to pollute the environment, and the «natural» waste was to be considered the actual source of contamination. More recently, the Club of Rome published their essay *The Limits of Growth*. As the OPEC had just increased the oil prices, the Club was under the spell of the limits of non-renewable natural resources and they wrote, «In any finite system, there must be constraints that can act to stop experimental growth». And they concluded, «We are searching for a model output that represents a world system that is:
1. Sustainable without sudden and uncontrollable collapse.
2. Capable of satisfying the basic material requirements of all his people».

In this conclusion, romanticism and rationalism go again hand to hand against markets to increase the role of loving and rational bureaucracies. I do not think that it is relevant now to analyze the price of oil under the light of the Club of Rome predictions.

Notwithstanding these antecedents and repetitive mistakes with respect to the predictions of global warming or freezing either one is immaterial from the point of view of bureaucratic interest in meddling into the production processes it appears that the concepts of «sustainable developments» and «precautionary principle» are here to stay. The policies based on those principles will necessarily reduce the standard of living in the industrial world, but worse than that they will prevent growth in the underdeveloped world. In that sense, it is necessary to take into account that the wealth of the industrial countries far from producing poverty is a fundamental premise of growth for the less developed countries. Hence, the elimination of risk that implies the precautionary principle prevents the technological change which is the only mean reason to improve human conditions around the world. In other words, the attempted salvation of the planet is to condemn humanity to poverty, which is the major pollutant in the world. The truth is that the private interest of bureaucracies collides with the private interest of humanity.

Thank you for acquiring

Rule of Law: The path to Freedom
from the
Stockcero collection of Spanish and Latin American significant books of the past and present.

This book is one of a large and ever-expanding list of titles Stockcero regards as classics of Spanish and Latin American literature, history, economics, and cultural studies. A series of important books are being brought back into print with modern readers and students in mind, and thus including updated footnotes, prefaces, and bibliographies.

We invite you to look for more complete information on our website, **www.stockcero.com**, where you can view a list of titles currently available, as well as those in preparation. On this website, you may register to receive desk copies, view additional information about the books, and suggest titles you would like to see brought back into print. We are most eager to receive these suggestions, and if possible, to discuss them with you. Any comments you wish to make about Stockcero books would be most helpful.

The Stockcero website will also provide access to an increasing number of links to critical articles, libraries, databanks, bibliographies and other materials relating to the texts we are publishing.

By registering on our website, you will allow us to inform you of services and connections that will enhance your reading and teaching of an expanding list of important books.

You may additionally help us improve the way we serve your needs by registering your purchase at:
http://www.stockcero.com/bookregister.htm

www.ingramcontent.com/pod-product-compliance
Lightning Source LLC
Chambersburg PA
CBHW021140230426
43667CB00005B/203